Mystic JUMBLE®

Puzzles to Bemuse and Bedazzle You!

Jeff Knurek,
Henri Arnold,
David L. Hoyt,
Bob Lee, &
Mike Argirion

TRIUMPH
BOOKS

This book is available in quantity at special discounts
for your group or organization.

For further information, contact:

Triumph Books LLC
814 North Franklin Street
Chicago, Illinois 60610
Phone: (312) 337-0747
www.triumphbooks.com

Printed in U.S.A.

ISBN: 978-1-62937-130-6

Design by Sue Knopf

Contents

Mystic JUMBLE

Classic Puzzles

JUMBLE®

Unscramble these four Jumbles, one letter to each square, to form four ordinary words.

DELOY

SELBS

MIRAPI

AFAIRS

WHERE THE GYMNAST FOUND THE MUSIC FOR HER ROUTINE.

Now arrange the circled letters to form the surprise answer, as suggested by the above cartoon.

Print answer here ON THE ⬡⬡⬡⬡⬡ ⬡⬡⬡⬡⬡

JUMBLE®

Unscramble these four Jumbles, one letter to each square, to form four ordinary words.

USAME

CYDER

KLEECH

BIRDHY

What are you doing here?

WHAT THE GUARD DID TO THE SHIP'S INTRUDER.

Now arrange the circled letters to form the surprise answer, as suggested by the above cartoon.

Print answer here HE ◯◯◯◯◯◯ ◯◯◯

3

JUMBLE®

Unscramble these four Jumbles, one letter to each square, to form four ordinary words.

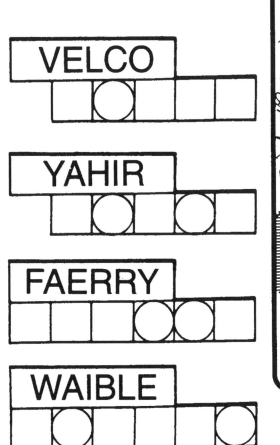

VELCO

YAHIR

FAERRY

WAIBLE

Let's get some more

SAMPLES

ANOTHER NAME FOR A GIVEAWAY.

Now arrange the circled letters to form the surprise answer, as suggested by the above cartoon.

Print answer here A "⬭⬭⬭⬭⬭" FOR ⬭⬭⬭

JUMBLE®

Unscramble these four Jumbles, one letter to
each square, to form four ordinary words.

STRUB

HOTOT

MOOBBA

TREMIC

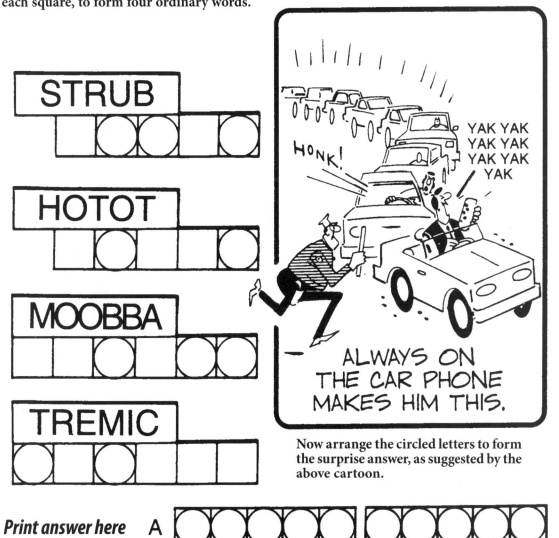

Now arrange the circled letters to form
the surprise answer, as suggested by the
above cartoon.

Print answer here A

JUMBLE®

Unscramble these four Jumbles, one letter to each square, to form four ordinary words.

ARGIN

TEVEN

GROHPE

STEFIA

WHAT ATTRACTED CUSTOMERS TO THE MATTRESS SHOP.

Now arrange the circled letters to form the surprise answer, as suggested by the above cartoon.

Print answer here " ◯◯◯◯◯◯◯ " ◯◯◯◯◯

JUMBLE®

Unscramble these four Jumbles, one letter to each square, to form four ordinary words.

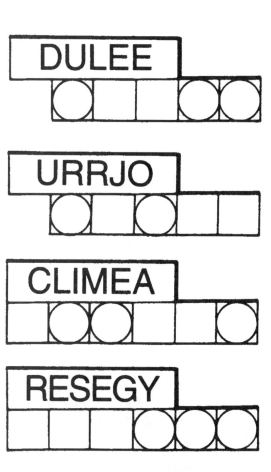

DULEE

URRJO

CLIMEA

RESEGY

A LOSING TEAM CAN TURN FANS INTO THIS.

Now arrange the circled letters to form the surprise answer, as suggested by the above cartoon.

Print answer here

JUMBLE

Unscramble these four Jumbles, one letter to
each square, to form four ordinary words.

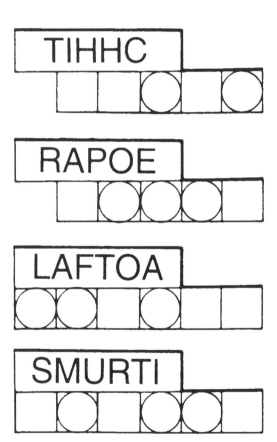

TIHHC

RAPOE

LAFTOA

SMURTI

WHAT THE
RANCHER WANTED
FROM HIS HERD.

Now arrange the circled letters to form
the surprise answer, as suggested by the
above cartoon.

*Print answer
here*

JUMBLE®

Unscramble these four Jumbles, one letter to each square, to form four ordinary words.

PEXLE

GOLIC

POLUCE

ALFELN

What was the time?

HOW THE TRAINER DETERMINED THE FASTEST HORSE.

Now arrange the circled letters to form the surprise answer, as suggested by the above cartoon.

Print answer here WITH A

JUMBLE®

Unscramble these four Jumbles, one letter to each square, to form four ordinary words.

RACCK

TELIT

THAGUT

TUFACE

Isn't he handsome?

WHAT SHE CONSIDERED HER ALL-STAR FIANCE.

Now arrange the circled letters to form the surprise answer, as suggested by the above cartoon.

Print answer here A

Unscramble these four Jumbles, one letter to each square, to form four ordinary words.

MUTAG

DABIE

NEEVEL

LIKLER

OCK BOTTOM PRICES

He's trying to snag customers

HOW THE FISHING SHOP ATTRACTED CUSTOMERS.

Now arrange the circled letters to form the surprise answer, as suggested by the above cartoon.

Print answer here IT ◯◯◯◯◯ ' ◯◯ ◯◯

JUMBLE®

Unscramble these four Jumbles, one letter to
each square, to form four ordinary words.

NIGIC

POATI

VOXCEN

CINTAG

We must be vigilant...

He really
sends me

WHAT THE
HAPPY-HOUR CROWD
CONSIDERED THE
ORATOR'S REMARKS.

Now arrange the circled letters to form
the surprise answer, as suggested by the
above cartoon.

**Print answer
here**

JUMBLE

Unscramble these four Jumbles, one letter to each square, to form four ordinary words.

TRAAP

CLEAB

MUJERP

FALACI

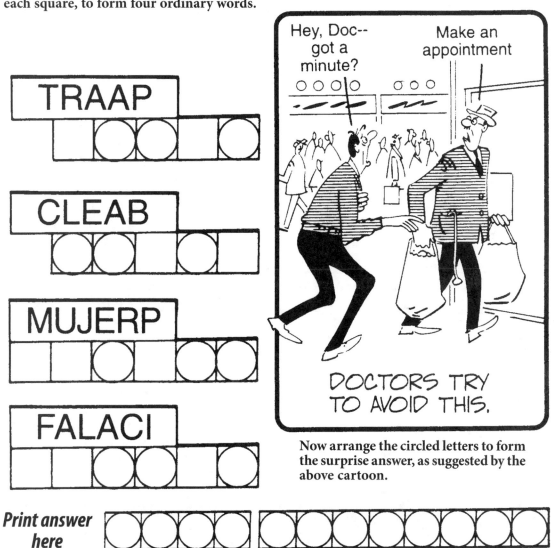

DOCTORS TRY TO AVOID THIS.

Now arrange the circled letters to form the surprise answer, as suggested by the above cartoon.

Print answer here

JUMBLE®

Unscramble these four Jumbles, one letter to each square, to form four ordinary words.

LOFEN

CUNEL

CRYLEE

HALINE

I'm taking one for the long march

THE BEST PART OF A SOLDIER'S MORNING.

Now arrange the circled letters to form the surprise answer, as suggested by the above cartoon.

Print answer here " ⬭⬭⬭⬭ " ⬭⬭⬭⬭

JUMBLE®

Unscramble these four Jumbles, one letter to
each square, to form four ordinary words.

KIHCT

TURET

YALSAW

BRICKE

After deductions, there's not much left

PAY

HE DREAMED
OF MILLIONS BUT
EVERY WEEK HE
RECEIVED THIS.

Now arrange the circled letters to form
the surprise answer, as suggested by the
above cartoon.

Print answer here A ⬡⬡⬡⬡⬡⬡⬡ ⬡⬡⬡⬡⬡⬡

JUMBLE®

Unscramble these four Jumbles, one letter to
each square, to form four ordinary words.

LAGIE

YURST

DONBEY

TELLMA

We're not as good
as we thought

ATHLETES WHO LEARN
HUMILITY OFTEN END
UP WITH THESE.

Now arrange the circled letters to form
the surprise answer, as suggested by the
above cartoon.

Print answer here

JUMBLE®

Unscramble these four Jumbles, one letter to each square, to form four ordinary words.

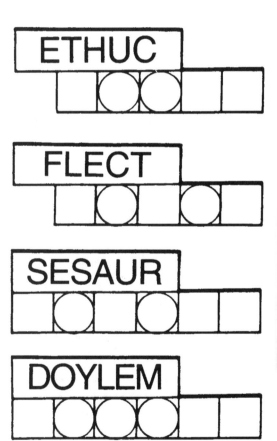

ETHUC

FLECT

SESAUR

DOYLEM

Can't squeeze another customer in here

FOR THE POKER PARLOR ALMOST NOTHING BEATS THIS.

Now arrange the circled letters to form the surprise answer, as suggested by the above cartoon.

Print answer here A ⬚⬚⬚⬚ ⬚⬚⬚⬚⬚

17

JUMBLE®

Unscramble these four Jumbles, one letter to
each square, to form four ordinary words.

GINTY

HAMER

MYNITE

PERUSH

It's the best
deal in town

10% ON
DEPOSITS

WHAT THE BANK GOT
FROM ITS FAVORABLE
YIELD OFFER.

Now arrange the circled letters to form
the surprise answer, as suggested by the
above cartoon.

**Print answer
here**

JUMBLE®

Unscramble these four Jumbles, one letter to
each square, to form four ordinary words.

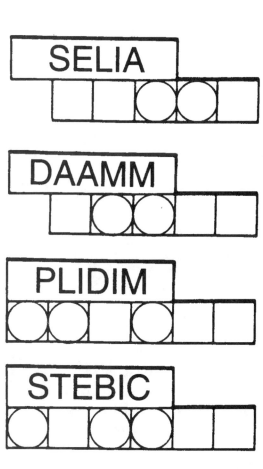

SELIA

DAAMM

PLIDIM

STEBIC

Who gets
this?

WHAT THE
LAWMAKERS DID
AT DINNER.

Now arrange the circled letters to form
the surprise answer, as suggested by the
above cartoon.

Print answer here ⬡⬡⬡⬡⬡⬡ THE ⬡⬡⬡⬡

JUMBLE®

Unscramble these four Jumbles, one letter to each square, to form four ordinary words.

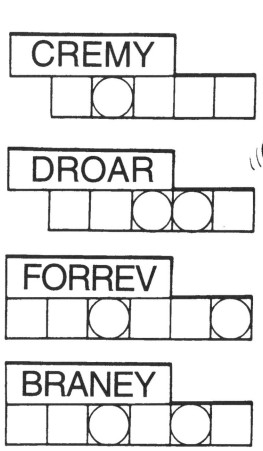

CREMY

DROAR

FORREV

BRANEY

I'll have some more potatoes

WHAT THE BOARDER WITH THE LONG REACH BECAME.

Now arrange the circled letters to form the surprise answer, as suggested by the above cartoon.

Print answer here

JUMBLE®

Unscramble these four Jumbles, one letter to
each square, to form four ordinary words.

SAYES

CITHY

RAYPER

DILEEY

We'll be landing in
a few minutes

WHAT THE
LAWYERS CALLED THE
FLIGHT UPDATE.

Now arrange the circled letters to form
the surprise answer, as suggested by the
above cartoon.

Print answer here " ☐☐☐☐☐ " ☐☐☐

JUMBLE®

Unscramble these four Jumbles, one letter to each square, to form four ordinary words.

ORBIL

WERFE

CHANIG

MEEBAC

WHAT MOTHER SAID TO THE BOY WHO HAD BEEN PLAYING WITH COAL.

Now arrange the circled letters to form the surprise answer, as suggested by the above cartoon.

Print answer here ☐☐☐☐☐ HAVE YOU " ☐☐☐ " ?

JUMBLE®

Unscramble these four Jumbles, one letter to each square, to form four ordinary words.

AGLEE

TUSEG

LYKING

SLUDOH

WHAT WAS
DR. JEKYLL'S
FAVORITE GAME?

Now arrange the circled letters to form the surprise answer, as suggested by the above cartoon.

Print answer here " ◯◯◯◯ " & ◯◯◯◯

JUMBLE®

Unscramble these four Jumbles, one letter to
each square, to form four ordinary words.

DOTUB

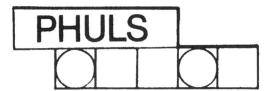

PHULS

GUBORE

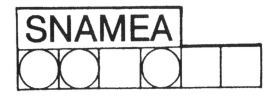

SNAMEA

WHAT THE MALE
OF THE SPECIES
WAS SUFFERING FROM
AS HE WAS ABOUT
TO GET MARRIED.

Now arrange the circled letters to form
the surprise answer, as suggested by the
above cartoon.

Print answer here

JUMBLE®

Unscramble these four Jumbles, one letter to each square, to form four ordinary words.

AZIME

KEDAB

PINGYT

ZAMONA

We've set the date!

LOVE MAY NOT MAKE THE WORLD GO ROUND, BUT IT CERTAINLY MAKES MANY PEOPLE THIS.

Now arrange the circled letters to form the surprise answer, as suggested by the above cartoon.

Print answer here

JUMBLE®

Unscramble these four Jumbles, one letter to
each square, to form four ordinary words.

ONIGG

LELOH

MILIES

DIBOUT

WHAT THAT
INGRATIATING BALD
GENTLEMAN WAS.

Now arrange the circled letters to form
the surprise answer, as suggested by the
above cartoon.

Print
answer AN
here

Mystic
JUMBLE®

Daily
Puzzles

JUMBLE®

Unscramble these four Jumbles, one letter to
each square, to form four ordinary words.

ELTAM

PONCA

UMRAIB

DEECCA

WHAT THE
OYSTER DID WHEN
ASKED WHERE ALL
HIS PEARLS WERE.

Now arrange the circled letters to form
the surprise answer, as suggested by the
above cartoon.

Print answer
here   HE "⬡⬡⬡⬡⬡⬡⬡⬡" ⬡⬡

JUMBLE®

Unscramble these four Jumbles, one letter to
each square, to form four ordinary words.

UNERP

LITUB

RECLAN

GIRLYS

THEY ALWAYS
TOOK THEIR FAT
UNCLE ALONG ON
DRIVES BECAUSE
OF WHAT HE HAD.

Now arrange the circled letters to form
the surprise answer, as suggested by the
above cartoon.

Print answer here A

JUMBLE

Unscramble these four Jumbles, one letter to each square, to form four ordinary words.

HEMRY

KORBO

TEELEY

BASHUM

Your husband?

SOME PEOPLE TELL JOKES AND OTHERS DO THIS.

Now arrange the circled letters to form the surprise answer, as suggested by the above cartoon.

Print answer here

JUMBLE®

Unscramble these four Jumbles, one letter to
each square, to form four ordinary words.

DUPON

YENAH

LISWEY

QUOMES

WHEN IT
COMES TO SHOES,
TIME DOES THIS.

Now arrange the circled letters to form
the surprise answer, as suggested by the
above cartoon.

*Print
answer
here*   ⬡⬡⬡⬡⬡ ALL ⬡⬡⬡⬡⬡

JUMBLE®

Unscramble these four Jumbles, one letter to each square, to form four ordinary words.

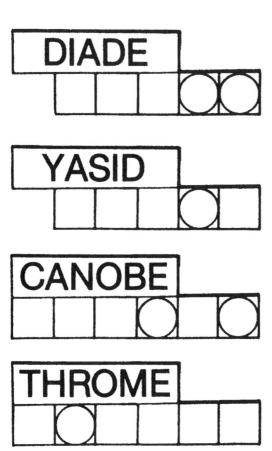

DIADE

YASID

CANOBE

THROME

Keep trying, keep trying

COACH

IF YOU DON'T SUCCEED AT FIRST, YOU'LL NEVER GET TO THIS.

Now arrange the circled letters to form the surprise answer, as suggested by the above cartoon.

Print answer here

JUMBLE®

Unscramble these four Jumbles, one letter to each square, to form four ordinary words.

EGGRO

FROOL

DIBEHN

ATVARC

HE BOUGHT A CAR WITHOUT A HORN BECAUSE HE DIDN'T THIS.

Now arrange the circled letters to form the surprise answer, as suggested by the above cartoon.

Print answer here  A

JUMBLE®

Unscramble these four Jumbles, one letter to each square, to form four ordinary words.

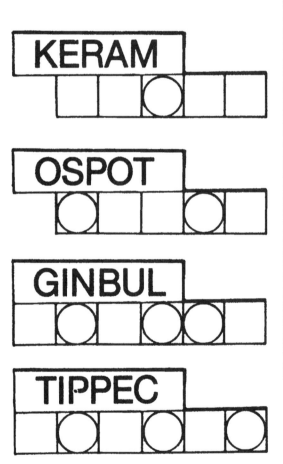

KERAM

OSPOT

GINBUL

TIPPEC

WHAT THE FAMILY WHO OWNED THE SWEATER FACTORY WAS.

Now arrange the circled letters to form the surprise answer, as suggested by the above cartoon.

Print answer here VERY

JUMBLE®

Unscramble these four Jumbles, one letter to each square, to form four ordinary words.

KICHT

NAGGI

CLAIFE

LIEROO

I guess I goofed

A MAN, WHO DOESN'T MIND ADMITTING HE'S "ALL WRONG" WHEN HE IS, IS THIS.

Now arrange the circled letters to form the surprise answer, as suggested by the above cartoon.

Print answer here

JUMBLE®

Unscramble these four Jumbles, one letter to each square, to form four ordinary words.

TAFAL

YAGUD

CLYMAL

BELUBB

You'll sleep like you never did before

WHAT THE SALESMAN SAID THAT BARGAIN BED WAS.

Now arrange the circled letters to form the surprise answer, as suggested by the above cartoon.

Print answer here A " ⬡⬡⬡⬡⬡⬡ – ⬡⬡⬡ "

JUMBLE®

Unscramble these four Jumbles, one letter to each square, to form four ordinary words.

GHEED

CHURS

CLIPES

SPIVLE

Doesn't have a brain in his head

WHAT HE WOULD BE IF HE SAID WHAT HE THOUGHT.

Now arrange the circled letters to form the surprise answer, as suggested by the above cartoon.

Print answer here

37

JUMBLE®

Unscramble these four Jumbles, one letter to
each square, to form four ordinary words.

ECOMA

GAPAN

GUNSLY

AMLAMM

There were no
human beings in
that country

WHERE DO
GOBLINS LIVE?

Now arrange the circled letters to form
the surprise answer, as suggested by the
above cartoon.

Print
answer   IN "◯◯◯◯◯" ◯◯◯'◯ LAND
here

Unscramble these four Jumbles, one letter to each square, to form four ordinary words.

MULAB

PHACT

NAWKEE

CLORLS

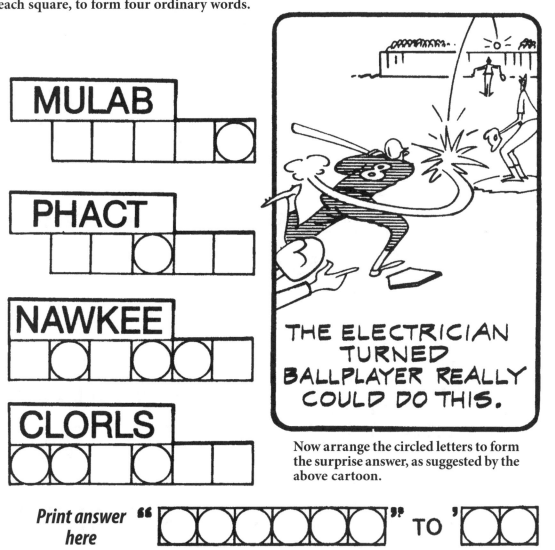

THE ELECTRICIAN TURNED BALLPLAYER REALLY COULD DO THIS.

Now arrange the circled letters to form the surprise answer, as suggested by the above cartoon.

Print answer here " ⬡⬡⬡⬡⬡⬡ " TO '⬡⬡

JUMBLE®

Unscramble these four Jumbles, one letter to
each square, to form four ordinary words.

PENTI

EPPIR

GREJIG

BAFLED

WHAT THE DENTIST
WHOSE INCOME
LAGGED BEHIND HIS
NEIGHBOR'S DECIDED
HE'D HAVE TO DO.

Now arrange the circled letters to form
the surprise answer, as suggested by the
above cartoon.

Print answer here ◯◯◯◯◯◯ THE ◯◯◯

JUMBLE®

Unscramble these four Jumbles, one letter to each square, to form four ordinary words.

BIBER

DIGUL

CALAPA

RUTUNE

HOW TO ENJOY READING A HORROR STORY.

Now arrange the circled letters to form the surprise answer, as suggested by the above cartoon.

Print answer here " ⬡⬡⬡⬡⬡⬡ " ⬡⬡⬡ WITH IT

JUMBLE®

Unscramble these four Jumbles, one letter to
each square, to form four ordinary words.

SLEBS

CUNOE

WARDTY

THROOC

HOW A NEST
EGG MUST
BE FEATHERED.

Now arrange the circled letters to form
the surprise answer, as suggested by the
above cartoon.

Print answer here WITH ⬡⬡⬡⬡ " ⬡⬡⬡⬡ "

JUMBLE®

Unscramble these four Jumbles, one letter to each square, to form four ordinary words.

TALGO

TESCA

ZEABAL

UPCATE

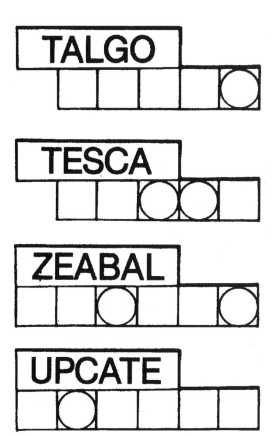

Let's cool it

THE MEMBERS OF THE JURY ARE SUPPOSED TO "SIT" UNTIL THEY DO THIS.

Now arrange the circled letters to form the surprise answer, as suggested by the above cartoon.

Print answer here "  "

JUMBLE®

Unscramble these four Jumbles, one letter to each square, to form four ordinary words.

VUMEA

LOVEH

BALTIR

SERVTY

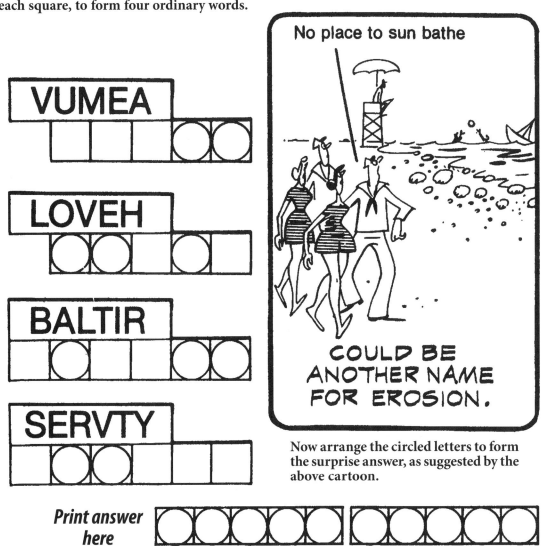

No place to sun bathe

COULD BE ANOTHER NAME FOR EROSION.

Now arrange the circled letters to form the surprise answer, as suggested by the above cartoon.

Print answer here

JUMBLE®

Unscramble these four Jumbles, one letter to each square, to form four ordinary words.

CHIRB

FELKA

INJOAD

BISCER

WHAT A MONUMENT IN THE PARK OFTEN REALLY IS.

Now arrange the circled letters to form the surprise answer, as suggested by the above cartoon.

Print answer here ⬡⬡⬡ THE ⬡⬡⬡⬡⬡

JUMBLE®

Unscramble these four Jumbles, one letter to each square, to form four ordinary words.

NORIG

CHOUP

WHAIGE

SELUNS

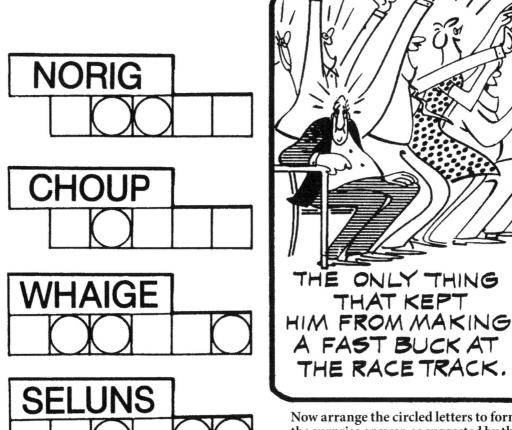

THE ONLY THING THAT KEPT HIM FROM MAKING A FAST BUCK AT THE RACE TRACK.

Now arrange the circled letters to form the surprise answer, as suggested by the above cartoon.

Print answer here A ☐☐☐☐☐ ☐☐☐☐☐☐

JUMBLE®

Unscramble these four Jumbles, one letter to
each square, to form four ordinary words.

WETTE

CHOLT

YAXLAG

NESING

HOW A COM-
PETENT THIEF
DOES HIS WORK.

Now arrange the circled letters to form
the surprise answer, as suggested by the
above cartoon.

Print
answer
here
" ☐☐☐☐☐ – ☐☐☐☐☐ "

47

PUZZLE 46

JUMBLE®

Unscramble these four Jumbles, one letter to each square, to form four ordinary words.

PHULS

NOIBS

VIQUER

TIVEHR

Did you think you could get away with THAT?

WHAT THE CUSTOMS INSPECTOR SAID THE SMUGGLER'S CASE WAS

Now arrange the circled letters to form the surprise answer, as suggested by the above cartoon.

Print answer here ◯◯◯◯ & ◯◯◯◯

48

Unscramble these four Jumbles, one letter to
each square, to form four ordinary words.

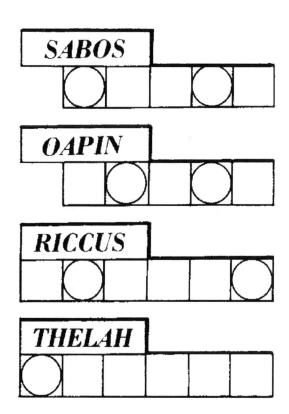

SABOS

OAPIN

RICCUS

THELAH

WHAT THEY CALLED
THE FOUNTAIN PEN
TYCOON.

Now arrange the circled letters to form
the surprise answer, as suggested by the
above cartoon.

Print answer here

JUMBLE.

Unscramble these four Jumbles, one letter to each square, to form four ordinary words.

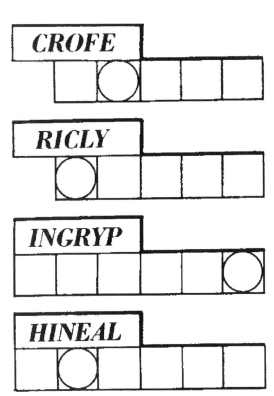

CROFE

RICLY

INGRYP

HINEAL

LATEST STYLES

WHAT THE PRUDE SAID MINISKIRTS COULDN'T BE WORN FOR.

Now arrange the circled letters to form the surprise answer, as suggested by the above cartoon.

Print answer here

50

JUMBLE

Unscramble these four Jumbles, one letter to
each square, to form four ordinary words.

NOCIT

GALEL

METHEL

PENOLY

MANY A GUY HAS
BEEN STUNG TRYING
TO GET THIS.

Now arrange the circled letters to form
the surprise answer, as suggested by the
above cartoon.

Print answer here **A**

51

JUMBLE®

Unscramble these four Jumbles, one letter to each square, to form four ordinary words.

RILLT

VAHEY

VIMOTE

GORUBE

HOW THE MISER HELD ON TO HIS DOUGH.

Now arrange the circled letters to form the surprise answer, as suggested by the above cartoon.

Print answer here

JUMBLE®

Unscramble these four Jumbles, one letter to
each square, to form four ordinary words.

BALEF

RAMEK

CLOPEM

NIXFUL

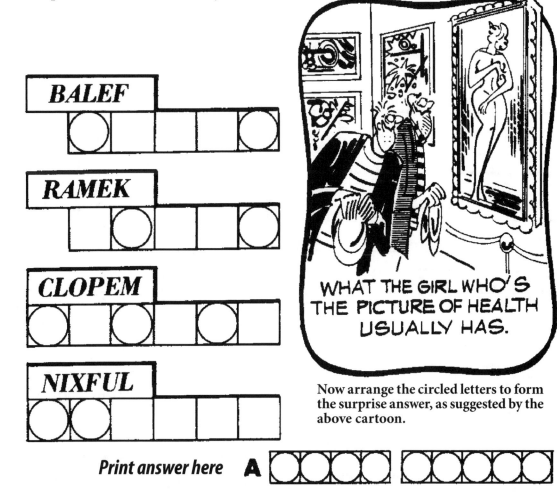

WHAT THE GIRL WHO'S
THE PICTURE OF HEALTH
USUALLY HAS.

Now arrange the circled letters to form
the surprise answer, as suggested by the
above cartoon.

Print answer here **A**

53

JUMBLE®

Unscramble these four Jumbles, one letter to
each square, to form four ordinary words.

PRUCO

SUJOT

TOSEFF

YURNEP

WHAT LADLES DO.

Now arrange the circled letters to form
the surprise answer, as suggested by the
above cartoon.

Print answer here

JUMBLE®

Unscramble these four Jumbles, one letter to each square, to form four ordinary words.

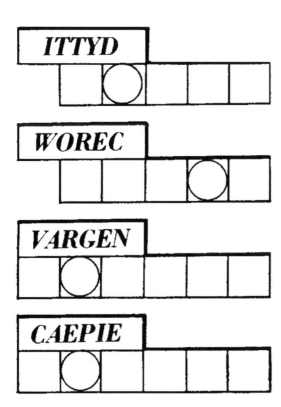

ITTYD

WOREC

VARGEN

CAEPIE

Come and get it!

READY TO EAT!

Now arrange the circled letters to form the surprise answer, as suggested by the above cartoon.

Print answer here

JUMBLE®

Unscramble these four Jumbles, one letter to
each square, to form four ordinary words.

DENUC

GRAWE

SERBIC

MIRVEN

THIS CAN PRODUCE
A TIGHT KIND
OF FEELING.

Now arrange the circled letters to form
the surprise answer, as suggested by the
above cartoon.

Print answer here **A**

JUMBLE®

Unscramble these four Jumbles, one letter to
each square, to form four ordinary words.

GARBE

ELLAD

MIGNIT

BILDOY

We're off to Philly
to see where it
was signed

DECLARATION
OF
INDEPENDENCE

IT'S ALL IT'S CRACKED
UP TO BE!

Now arrange the circled letters to form
the surprise answer, as suggested by the
above cartoon.

**Print answer
here** **THE** ⭕⭕⭕⭕⭕⭕⭕ ⭕⭕⭕⭕

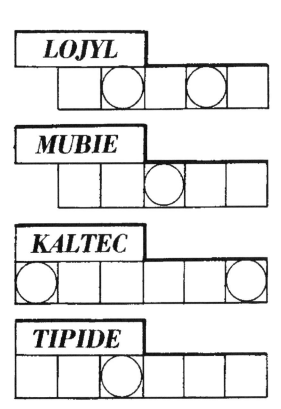

JUMBLE®

Unscramble these four Jumbles, one letter to
each square, to form four ordinary words.

LOJYL

MUBIE

KALTEC

TIPIDE

YE TAVERN

CLOSED

WHEN OPEN, IT
PROVIDES DRINKS.

Now arrange the circled letters to form
the surprise answer, as suggested by the
above cartoon.

Print answer here **A**

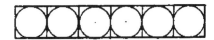

58

JUMBLE®

Unscramble these four Jumbles, one letter to each square, to form four ordinary words.

Instead of George, I think I'll see Harold tonight

WHEN YOU MIGHT DECIDE TO CHANGE A DATE.

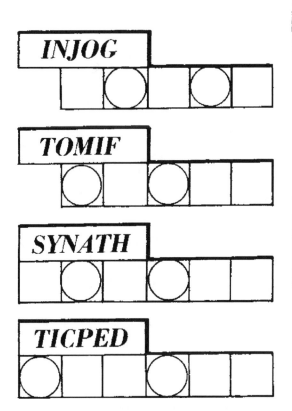

INJOG

TOMIF

SYNATH

TICPED

Now arrange the circled letters to form the surprise answer, as suggested by the above cartoon.

Print answer here **AT** ◯◯◯◯◯◯◯◯

JUMBLE®

Unscramble these four Jumbles, one letter to
each square, to form four ordinary words.

SALIE

RETEX

MUGNIP

NACTAV

There's another
sale we'll skip

FURS

NOW!!
ONLY $25,000

ONE THING YOU
CAN SAY FOR
BEING POOR.

Now arrange the circled letters to form
the surprise answer, as suggested by the
above cartoon.

Print answer here **IT'S** ⬡⬡⬡⬡⬡⬡⬡⬡⬡⬡⬡⬡

JUMBLE®

Unscramble these four Jumbles, one letter to each square, to form four ordinary words.

INBAC

UDGIE

BELJUM

HUMILE

WOW!

HOW THE MAGISTRATE WHO WAS PLAYING TRUANT IN THE PARK ACTED.

Now arrange the circled letters to form the surprise answer, as suggested by the above cartoon.

Print answer here

LIKE A ⬡⬡⬡⬡⬡ ON THE ⬡⬡⬡⬡⬡

JUMBLE®

Unscramble these four Jumbles, one letter to
each square, to form four ordinary words.

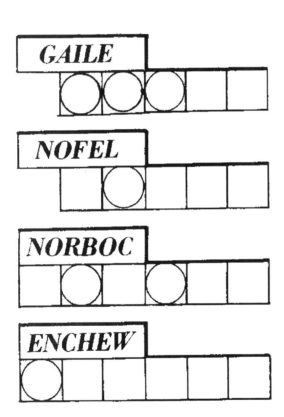

GAILE

NOFEL

NORBOC

ENCHEW

Here are a few more

WHAT THE MODEL'S
JOB WAS.

Now arrange the circled letters to form
the surprise answer, as suggested by the
above cartoon.

Print answer here

JUMBLE®

Unscramble these four Jumbles, one letter to
each square, to form four ordinary words.

DYRYL

OINES

GATHIL

HINCLE

Let's borrow
from Grandpa

THESE KIDS MIGHT
MAKE *THE RICH LEND.*

Now arrange the circled letters to form
the surprise answer, as suggested by the
above cartoon.

Print answer here **THE** ◯◯◯◯◯◯◯◯◯

JUMBLE®

Unscramble these four Jumbles, one letter to
each square, to form four ordinary words.

LAVEE

NOYME

HERLAW

WAHLIE

It looks better now

WHAT THE RAKE WAS
TURNED INTO AFTER HE
GOT MARRIED.

Now arrange the circled letters to form
the surprise answer, as suggested by the
above cartoon.

Print answer here **A**

JUMBLE®

Unscramble these four Jumbles, one letter to each square, to form four ordinary words.

WERFE

TIPEY

YIMTID

MUBBEN

WHY THE RAM
STOPPED IN HIS
TRACKS.

Now arrange the circled letters to form the surprise answer, as suggested by the above cartoon.

Print answer here **HE SAW A** ◯◯◯ ◯◯◯◯

JUMBLE®

Unscramble these four Jumbles, one letter to
each square, to form four ordinary words.

TARAL

ECTAN

UNBEAT

WENTIG

Will it be a boy or a girl?

YOU DON'T KNOW
IF YOU'RE THIS!

Now arrange the circled letters to form
the surprise answer, as suggested by the
above cartoon.

Print answer here

JUMBLE®

Unscramble these four Jumbles, one letter to each square, to form four ordinary words.

PEWID

TRAFE

HOMIDS

YARNLE

WHAT HE THOUGHT HIS WIFE'S MOTHER WAS.

Now arrange the circled letters to form the surprise answer, as suggested by the above cartoon.

Print answer here A ⟨◯◯◯◯◯◯◯⟩ - ⟨◯◯⟩ - ⟨◯◯◯⟩

JUMBLE®

Unscramble these four Jumbles, one letter to each square, to form four ordinary words.

TIFED

GLOIC

HINSAV

LARBUT

CRASH!!

That does it!

BROKEN HOMES

HOW MODERN HOUSE-WIVES SOMETIMES GET RID OF UNSATIS-FACTORY DISHWASHERS.

Now arrange the circled letters to form the surprise answer, as suggested by the above cartoon.

Print answer here **THEY** ⬡⬡⬡⬡⬡⬡⬡ **'EM**

JUMBLE®

Unscramble these four Jumbles, one letter to
each square, to form four ordinary words.

SEROU

LAFAT

NEEBOG

STANEF

They HAD to promote me—I've always done the IMPORTANT things around here

TO FILL A BIG MAN'S SHOES YOU WOULDN'T DO THIS.

Now arrange the circled letters to form
the surprise answer, as suggested by the
above cartoon.

*Print
answer
here* ◯◯◯◯ **ABOUT YOUR** ◯◯◯◯◯

JUMBLE®

Unscramble these four Jumbles, one letter to
each square, to form four ordinary words.

(Puff)

Ready for
the workout?

TRAINER

FOR SOME PEOPLE,
WEIGHT LIFTING
MIGHT MEAN THIS.

LUDGI

TOSOP

NAITAT

PAMEND

Now arrange the circled letters to form
the surprise answer, as suggested by the
above cartoon.

Print answer here

JUMBLE®

Unscramble these four Jumbles, one letter to
each square, to form four ordinary words.

HINKT

ROYAF

FAIRAS

SACCES

THIS MIGHT BE
CONSPICUOUS IN SOME
UNDERWATER PLAY.

Now arrange the circled letters to form
the surprise answer, as suggested by the
above cartoon.

Print answer here **A**

71

JUMBLE®

Unscramble these four Jumbles, one letter to
each square, to form four ordinary words.

ILEEX

MARFE

ANIZIN

TALFOA

WHAT A MOROCCAN
SAID TO SOMEONE
HE HADN'T SEEN
IN YEARS.

Now arrange the circled letters to form
the surprise answer, as suggested by the
above cartoon.

Print
answer
here

YOUR ⬡⬡⬡ IS ⬡⬡⬡⬡⬡⬡⬡⬡⬡

JUMBLE®

Unscramble these four Jumbles, one letter to each square, to form four ordinary words.

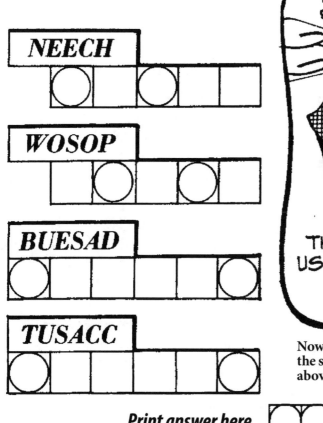

NEECH

WOSOP

BUESAD

TUSACC

From the finest geese

PAY NOW AND $AVE

JUST MARRIED

THE BEST THING TO USE FOR FEATHERING YOUR NEST.

Now arrange the circled letters to form the surprise answer, as suggested by the above cartoon.

Print answer here

73

JUMBLE®

Unscramble these four Jumbles, one letter to each square, to form four ordinary words.

RYPAH

KANTE

YERSIM

RYLAIF

What do you think?

WHAT THE GUY WHO CLAIMED HE COULD READ WOMEN LIKE A BOOK MUST HAVE BEEN.

Now arrange the circled letters to form the surprise answer, as suggested by the above cartoon.

Print answer here **A** ⬚⬚⬚⬚⬚⬚⬚ ⬚⬚⬚

JUMBLE®

Unscramble these four Jumbles, one letter to each square, to form four ordinary words.

VELOC

REESA

CLAGEY

RAVEEB

HOW THE REDUCING BUSINESS IS CARRIED ON.

Now arrange the circled letters to form the surprise answer, as suggested by the above cartoon.

Print answer here **ON A** ⬡⬡⬡⬡⬡ ⬡⬡⬡⬡⬡

JUMBLE®

Unscramble these four Jumbles, one letter to each square, to form four ordinary words.

CUHLG

PLEEX

DOAJIN

INDURG

Mmm—nice breakfast

STOLEN FROM A CHICKEN FARM.

Now arrange the circled letters to form the surprise answer, as suggested by the above cartoon.

Print answer here A " ⃝⃝⃝⃝⃝⃝⃝ " ⃝⃝⃝

JUMBLE®

Unscramble these four Jumbles, one letter to each square, to form four ordinary words.

RUPUS

GEREM

BABFLY

STEJER

This is where it's at

CURRENTLY INFLUENTIAL AROUND THE SOUTH-EASTERN U.S. COAST.

Now arrange the circled letters to form the surprise answer, as suggested by the above cartoon.

Print answer here **THE** ⬡⬡⬡⬡⬡ ⬡⬡⬡⬡⬡⬡

77

JUMBLE®

Unscramble these four Jumbles, one letter to each square, to form four ordinary words.

WIHSS

NOYOL

LENKEN

RIFUGE

GIRLS SHOULD NEVER LET A FOOL KISS THEM — OR THIS.

Now arrange the circled letters to form the surprise answer, as suggested by the above cartoon.

Print answer here **A** ☐☐☐☐☐ ☐☐☐☐☐ **THEM**

JUMBLE®

Unscramble these four Jumbles, one letter to
each square, to form four ordinary words.

IGSEE

MEHRY

MODEOD

SHEARE

Great meal

HOW TO PUT THE
BOSS IN A
GOOD HUMOR.

Now arrange the circled letters to form
the surprise answer, as suggested by the
above cartoon.

Print answer here ☐☐ THE ☐☐☐☐☐☐☐ FOR ☐☐☐

79

JUMBLE®

Unscramble these four Jumbles, one letter to each square, to form four ordinary words.

TIGAN

UNGLE

ENGLUP

CATNIG

THE KIND OF GUYS MANY GALS LOOK FOR.

Now arrange the circled letters to form the surprise answer, as suggested by the above cartoon.

Print answer here ⟨◯◯◯◯◯◯◯◯⟩ **ONES**

JUMBLE®

Unscramble these four Jumbles, one letter to
each square, to form four ordinary words.

SHURC

UNERP

GLUBIN

SIMDAL

WHEN YOU'RE THIS
IT'S EASY TO
FEEL CHIPPER.

Now arrange the circled letters to form
the surprise answer, as suggested by the
above cartoon.

Print answer here ◯◯ **THE** ◯◯◯◯◯

JUMBLE®

Unscramble these four Jumbles, one letter to each square, to form four ordinary words.

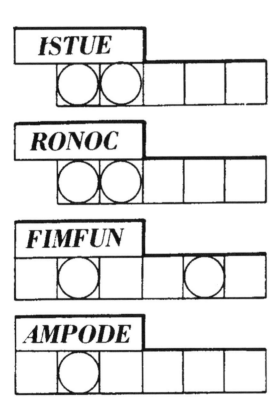

ISTUE

RONOC

FIMFUN

AMPODE

WHAT YOU SOMETIMES GET WHEN YOU PUT TWO AND TWO TOGETHER.

Now arrange the circled letters to form the surprise answer, as suggested by the above cartoon.

Print answer here

82

JUMBLE®

Unscramble these four Jumbles, one letter to
each square, to form four ordinary words.

KANEO

TOTID

BRATIL

CUNNEA

How old? — Shhh!

THE BEST WAY TO TELL
A WOMAN'S AGE.

Now arrange the circled letters to form
the surprise answer, as suggested by the
above cartoon.

Print
answer
here
WHEN SHE'S ◯◯◯ ◯◯◯◯◯◯

JUMBLE®

Unscramble these four Jumbles, one letter to
each square, to form four ordinary words.

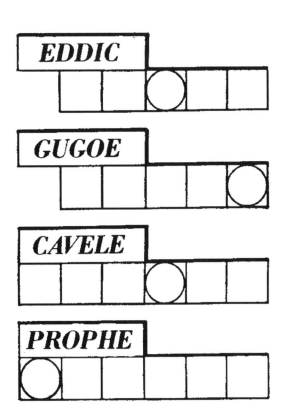

EDDIC

GUGOE

CAVELE

PROPHE

EACH WITH A PAIN.

Now arrange the circled letters to form
the surprise answer, as suggested by the
above cartoon.

Print answer here

JUMBLE®

Unscramble these four Jumbles, one letter to
each square, to form four ordinary words.

IVGLI

ARSYC

HIRTED

ATTARR

Back
to
work!

A DRESS SHOULD
BE THIS WHEN IT'S
ATTRACTIVE.

Now arrange the circled letters to form
the surprise answer, as suggested by the
above cartoon.

Print answer here

JUMBLE®

Unscramble these four Jumbles, one letter to
each square, to form four ordinary words.

PIDEB

DELOY

TRUVIE

VOONCY

THIS LEAVES
NO ONE OUT!

Now arrange the circled letters to form
the surprise answer, as suggested by the
above cartoon.

Print answer here

JUMBLE®

Unscramble these four Jumbles, one letter to
each square, to form four ordinary words.

YAFLE

VIILC

DILVER

MAIDDY

WHAT SOME DENTISTS
MIGHT GIVE YOU.

Now arrange the circled letters to form
the surprise answer, as suggested by the
above cartoon.

Print
answer
here
THE ⬡⬡⬡⬡⬡⬡ OF YOUR ⬡⬡⬡⬡

JUMBLE®

Unscramble these four Jumbles, one letter to each square, to form four ordinary words.

PEELO

TEJCE

MATARU

GUNFEL

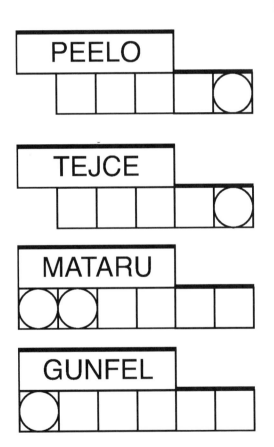

I think I'll buy this for my yard.

Let me buy this for you. You helped me install my fence last week and it would be my pleasure to buy this oak for you.

HE PAID FOR HIS NEIGHBOR'S NEW OAK BECAUSE HE WANTED TO ---

Now arrange the circled letters to form the surprise answer, as suggested by the above cartoon.

Print answer here " ⬡⬡⬡⬡⬡ "

JUMBLE®

Unscramble these four Jumbles, one letter to each square, to form four ordinary words.

GOMIZ

MOTEP

NAPXED

NEYROD

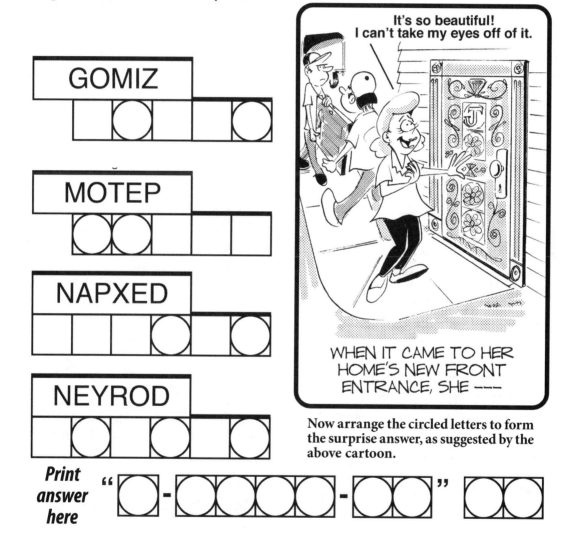

It's so beautiful!
I can't take my eyes off of it.

WHEN IT CAME TO HER HOME'S NEW FRONT ENTRANCE, SHE ----

Now arrange the circled letters to form the surprise answer, as suggested by the above cartoon.

Print answer here " ☐-☐☐☐☐-☐☐ " ☐☐

JUMBLE

Unscramble these four Jumbles, one letter to each square, to form four ordinary words.

DUWEN

WORLP

NEYGAC

GRITFH

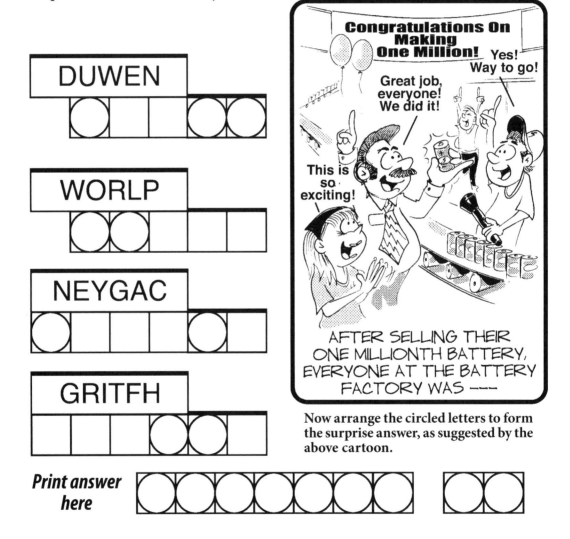

Congratulations On Making One Million!

Yes! Way to go!

Great job, everyone! We did it!

This is so exciting!

AFTER SELLING THEIR ONE MILLIONTH BATTERY, EVERYONE AT THE BATTERY FACTORY WAS ---

Now arrange the circled letters to form the surprise answer, as suggested by the above cartoon.

Print answer here

JUMBLE®

Unscramble these four Jumbles, one letter to each square, to form four ordinary words.

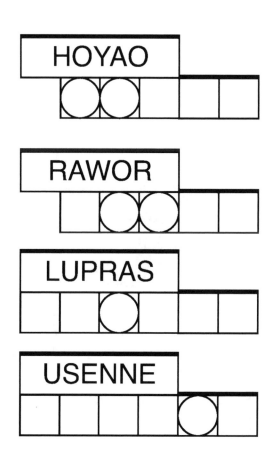

HOYAO

RAWOR

LUPRAS

USENNE

THE STEAKS AT THE CHEF'S TOP-RATED RESTAURANT WERE UNDERCOOKED ---

Now arrange the circled letters to form the surprise answer, as suggested by the above cartoon.

Print answer here

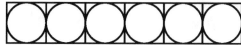

JUMBLE®

Unscramble these four Jumbles, one letter to
each square, to form four ordinary words.

CAREZ

THIGF

TOPNUW

CIXTEO

Why run,
when you can
walk?

Are you blind?
How could you call
that a ball? I threw it
right over the plate!

AFTER HE WALKED HOME
THE WINNING RUN, THE
PITCHER ---

Now arrange the circled letters to form
the surprise answer, as suggested by the
above cartoon.

*Print
answer
here*

JUMBLE®

Unscramble these four Jumbles, one letter to each square, to form four ordinary words.

KESAD

PUYSO

LARFOL

AUBERU

THE WRESTLER ON THE BOTTOM WAS GOING TO END UP BEING A ----

Now arrange the circled letters to form the surprise answer, as suggested by the above cartoon.

Print answer here

JUMBLE®

Unscramble these four Jumbles, one letter to
each square, to form four ordinary words.

VETEN

THENT

KAEEUR

PAMELI

This rock
is harder
than I
expected!

If we keep
digging
here, we'll
find ice.

THE ASTRONAUTS ON
MARS DUG FOR ICE IN AN
ATTEMPT TO ----

Now arrange the circled letters to form
the surprise answer, as suggested by the
above cartoon.

*Print answer
here*

JUMBLE®

Unscramble these four Jumbles, one letter to each square, to form four ordinary words.

CHETI

LETYS

ROMRAY

YAVIRA

Kraken's department has increased sinkings by 60%.

IF THE OCEAN WERE RUN BY A CORPORATION, THEN POSEIDON COULD BE THE ---

Now arrange the circled letters to form the surprise answer, as suggested by the above cartoon.

Print answer here " ◯◯◯ " ◯.◯.

JUMBLE®

Unscramble these four Jumbles, one letter to each square, to form four ordinary words.

SOBYS

TOLCH

GINKTH

NIFTIE

Morning! How are you feeling today?

I'm ready for this flu to go away.

AFTER HAVING THE FLU FOR A WEEK, SHE WAS ---

Now arrange the circled letters to form the surprise answer, as suggested by the above cartoon.

Print answer here

JUMBLE®

Unscramble these four Jumbles, one letter to each square, to form four ordinary words.

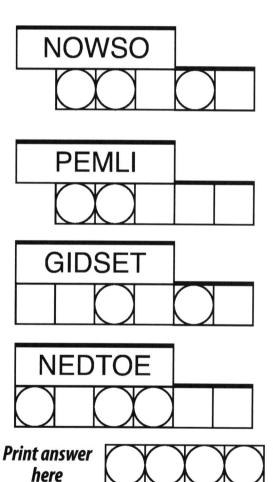

NOWSO

PEMLI

GIDSET

NEDTOE

Print answer here

He's not very consistent today.

Well, at least he had a great drive.

Rats!

THE ERRATIC GOLFER WAS EXPERIENCING ---

Now arrange the circled letters to form the surprise answer, as suggested by the above cartoon.

JUMBLE®

Unscramble these four Jumbles, one letter to each square, to form four ordinary words.

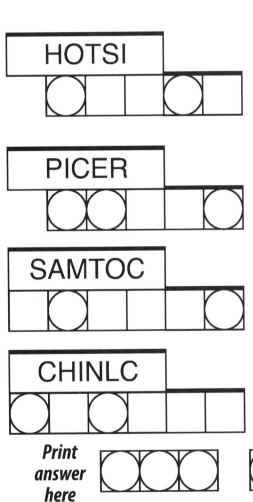

HOTSI

PICER

SAMTOC

CHINLC

It looks like apple outsold cherry and blueberry this month.

I can see why it's such a big slice of our revenue.

THE OWNER OF THE SUCCESSFUL BAKERY LIKED TO SHOW OFF HER – – –

Now arrange the circled letters to form the surprise answer, as suggested by the above cartoon.

Print answer here

JUMBLE®

Unscramble these four Jumbles, one letter to each square, to form four ordinary words.

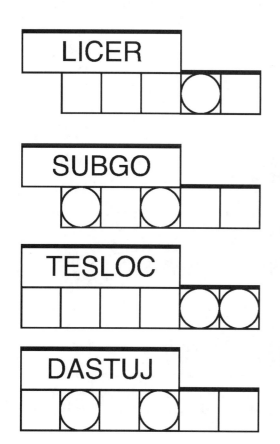

LICER

SUBGO

TESLOC

DASTUJ

I have to figure out how to get this bill paid. I've got to cut back on shopping.

This is so cute. I'll buy it from you if that will help.

SHE TRIED TO MAKE A DENT IN HER CREDIT CARD DEBT, BUT SHE COULDN'T ----

Now arrange the circled letters to form the surprise answer, as suggested by the above cartoon.

Print answer here

JUMBLE

Unscramble these four Jumbles, one letter to
each square, to form four ordinary words.

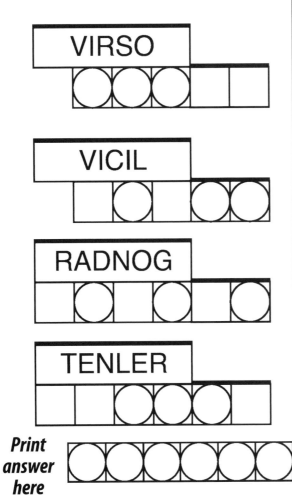

VIRSO

VICIL

RADNOG

TENLER

Well, at least we
can turn this into
sterling.

It's not
a total loss.

THE GOLD MINE TURNED
OUT TO BE A BUST, BUT
THANKFULLY, THERE
WAS A ---

Now arrange the circled letters to form
the surprise answer, as suggested by the
above cartoon.

**Print
answer
here**

JUMBLE®

Unscramble these four Jumbles, one letter to each square, to form four ordinary words.

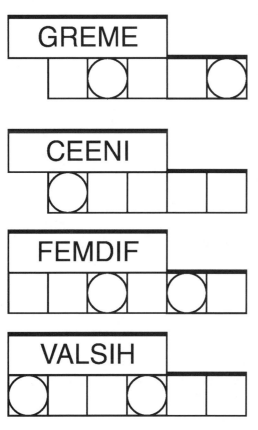

GREME

CEENI

FEMDIF

VALSIH

This is going to be grrreat!

The tickets are my treat.

ADMISSIONS

$5

WHEN THE CATS WAITED TO ENTER THE AMUSEMENT PARK, THEY STOOD IN A ---

Now arrange the circled letters to form the surprise answer, as suggested by the above cartoon.

Print answer here " ◯◯◯ - ◯◯◯◯ "

101

JUMBLE®

Unscramble these four Jumbles, one letter to each square, to form four ordinary words.

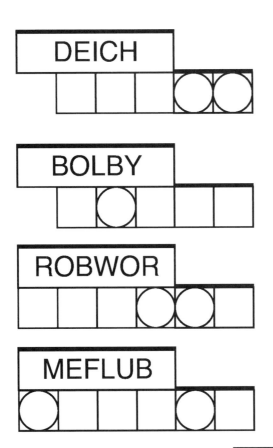

DEICH

BOLBY

ROBWOR

MEFLUB

ALL OAK 80% OFF!

This is our best price of the year.

Oh, my gosh! It's like you're giving this away.

WHEN HE SAW THE PRICE OF THE HARDWOOD, HE WAS ----

Now arrange the circled letters to form the surprise answer, as suggested by the above cartoon.

Print answer here

JUMBLE®

Unscramble these four Jumbles, one letter to each square, to form four ordinary words.

PLACM

LIWTL

CIWDEK

ROJNAG

Hurry up! I'm only in here for 10 years.

Wrap it up!

That's great, honey. Could you put Junior on the phone?

THE PHONE AT THE PRISON FEATURED – – –

Now arrange the circled letters to form the surprise answer, as suggested by the above cartoon.

Print answer here

JUMBLE®

Unscramble these four Jumbles, one letter to
each square, to form four ordinary words.

PMETT

ENOMY

SKURNH

CANYUL

Hey, honey. Did you
read this article about
how the U.S. may get
rid of the penny? It will
help the economy.

That's
ridiculous.

SHE THOUGHT THE IDEA
OF ELIMINATING THE PENNY
WAS ---

Now arrange the circled letters to form
the surprise answer, as suggested by the
above cartoon.

Print answer "◯◯◯-◯◯◯◯◯"
here

JUMBLE®

Unscramble these four Jumbles, one letter to each square, to form four ordinary words.

SLYYH

GEEWD

SLOMBY

MINLEB

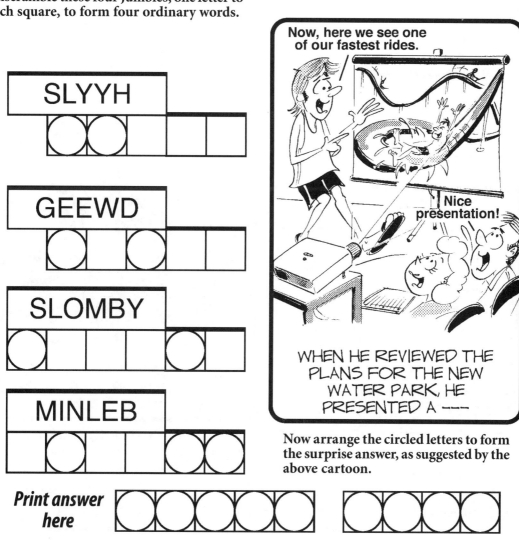

Now, here we see one of our fastest rides.

Nice presentation!

WHEN HE REVIEWED THE PLANS FOR THE NEW WATER PARK, HE PRESENTED A ----

Now arrange the circled letters to form the surprise answer, as suggested by the above cartoon.

Print answer here ◯◯◯◯◯ ◯◯◯◯

JUMBLE®

Unscramble these four Jumbles, one letter to
each square, to form four ordinary words.

TIYKT

SUREH

CISNEK

NADTET

I knew just
when to do
that to keep
them away.

Nice
job,
Mom.

THE SKUNK KNEW EXACTLY
WHEN TO SPRAY, BECAUSE
SHE HAD GOOD ----

Now arrange the circled letters to form
the surprise answer, as suggested by the
above cartoon.

Print answer here " ⬭⬭ - ⬭⬭⬭⬭⬭⬭ "

JUMBLE®

Unscramble these four Jumbles, one letter to
each square, to form four ordinary words.

UBOTA

LEEUD

GLLAEE

DOLBIY

I want to
know where
you were!
Now talk!

We have to let
him go. His story
checks out.

I'm out
of here.
C-ya!

HE WOULD BE LEAVING THE
POLICE STATION WITHOUT
BEING CHARGED, THANKS
TO AN ----

Now arrange the circled letters to form
the surprise answer, as suggested by the
above cartoon.

Print answer here " ☐◯◯◯ - ◯◯◯ "

JUMBLE®

Unscramble these four Jumbles, one letter to
each square, to form four ordinary words.

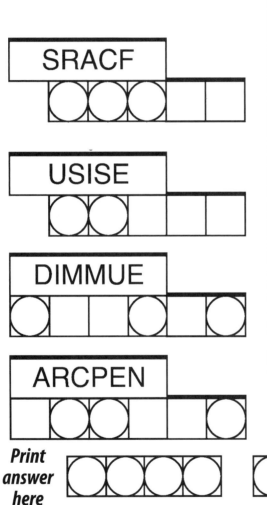

SRACF

USISE

DIMMUE

ARCPEN

**Print
answer
here**

What?! They have
different plugs here!
I'm going to be late!
I'm so jet-lagged.

WHEN THE BEAUTY PAGEANT
WINNER FROM THE U.S.
TRAVELED, SOMETIMES SHE
WOULD ---

Now arrange the circled letters to form
the surprise answer, as suggested by the
above cartoon.

JUMBLE®

Unscramble these four Jumbles, one letter to
each square, to form four ordinary words.

SIJOT

BACAK

CEDTOK

CYOPPH

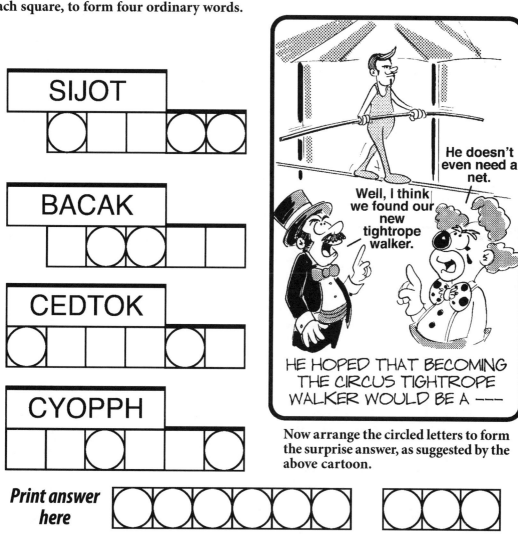

He doesn't
even need a
net.

Well, I think
we found our
new
tightrope
walker.

HE HOPED THAT BECOMING
THE CIRCUS TIGHTROPE
WALKER WOULD BE A ----

Now arrange the circled letters to form
the surprise answer, as suggested by the
above cartoon.

**Print answer
here**

JUMBLE®

Unscramble these four Jumbles, one letter to each square, to form four ordinary words.

HALSS

SIRYK

ROSDUH

TIKNET

HIS POOR JUDGMENT WHEN IT CAME TO DESIGNING TANK TOPS WOULD CAUSE HIM TO ---

Now arrange the circled letters to form the surprise answer, as suggested by the above cartoon.

Print answer here

JUMBLE®

Unscramble these four Jumbles, one letter to each square, to form four ordinary words.

RUPEN

YINOR

GAUTOE

WORDYS

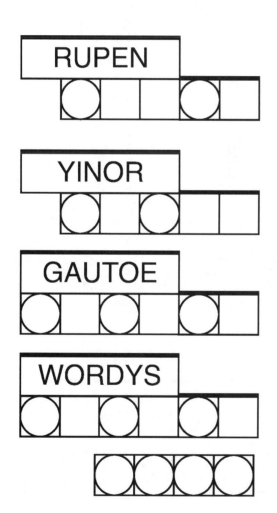

You can fish with it. You can hunt with it. And when using it as a weapon, you can keep a safe distance away. You can't do any of that with a club.

Ugg!

B.C.'s Spears New and Used

WHEN HE TALKED ABOUT THE ADVANTAGES OF USING A SPEAR, HE MADE SOME ---

Now arrange the circled letters to form the surprise answer, as suggested by the above cartoon.

JUMBLE®

Unscramble these four Jumbles, one letter to each square, to form four ordinary words.

SACEE

GUNYO

MOSHOC

WANOPE

Can this go out with the regular trash?

I'm not getting any sleep. That cat's upset. I didn't know Vivian would need so many diapers.

THE ARRIVAL OF THE NEW BABY BROUGHT ---

Now arrange the circled letters to form the surprise answer, as suggested by the above cartoon.

Print answer here

Unscramble these four Jumbles, one letter to
each square, to form four ordinary words.

NEESS

ENAGT

RIGCAL

AZETOL

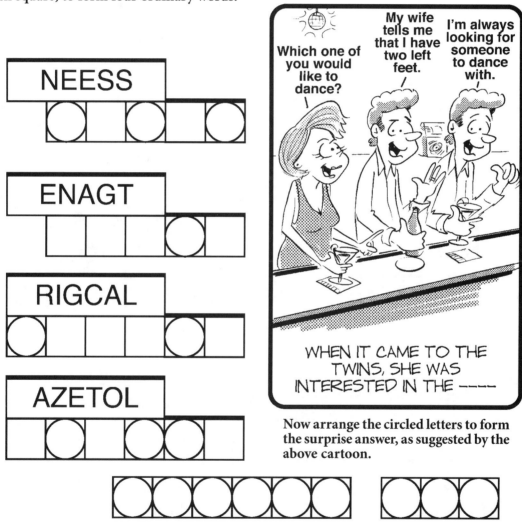

Which one of
you would
like to
dance?

My wife
tells me
that I have
two left
feet.

I'm always
looking for
someone
to dance
with.

WHEN IT CAME TO THE
TWINS, SHE WAS
INTERESTED IN THE ----

Now arrange the circled letters to form
the surprise answer, as suggested by the
above cartoon.

JUMBLE®

Unscramble these four Jumbles, one letter to each square, to form four ordinary words.

LETUF

CIUJE

DOMSET

KRINSH

What is this?
I haven't had hair like
that in 20 years.

THE JUDGE'S
PORTRAIT
DIDN'T ---

Now arrange the circled letters to form the surprise answer, as suggested by the above cartoon.

Print answer here

114

Unscramble these four Jumbles, one letter to each square, to form four ordinary words.

SEYZT

CHITK

DACIEV

NIMLEG

HE PLAYED CHESS IN PRAGUE WITH HIS ---

Now arrange the circled letters to form the surprise answer, as suggested by the above cartoon.

Print answer here " ◯◯◯◯◯ " ◯◯◯◯

JUMBLE®

Unscramble these four Jumbles, one letter to each square, to form four ordinary words.

TYPTE

KEREC

REHYOT

OJILAV

If you wanted pepperoni, you should have ordered pepperoni.

All right. Enough arguing. Let's call a truce. I'll give you a slice of my pizza if you give me a slice of yours.

THE ARGUMENT ABOUT THE PIZZAS ENDED WITH A ---

Now arrange the circled letters to form the surprise answer, as suggested by the above cartoon.

Print answer here

"◯◯◯◯◯" ◯◯◯◯◯◯

JUMBLE

Unscramble these four Jumbles, one letter to each square, to form four ordinary words.

INSUM

AOFTO

LATLEB

SHTECK

Jeff, would you like some pumpkin pie?

I can't eat another bite, Mom. I'm so glad we could all be together today.

AFTER THE HUGE TURKEY DINNER WITH THE FAMILY, HE WAS ----

Now arrange the circled letters to form the surprise answer, as suggested by the above cartoon.

Print answer here " ☐☐☐☐☐ - ☐☐☐☐ "

JUMBLE®

Unscramble these four Jumbles, one letter to each square, to form four ordinary words.

NAGIT

TLAVE

DUIPAN

DAMYID

Now everybody can see our information from miles around.

Money well spent.

ANN'S HOUSE OF HUMMELS NEXT EXIT

visit MAC'S ANTIQUE MALL

Bill's Hauss of Curiosity's

SHE HOPED HER NEW BILLBOARD WOULD GIVE HER COMPANY ONE.

Now arrange the circled letters to form the surprise answer, as suggested by the above cartoon.

Print answer here AN ◯◯-◯◯◯◯◯◯◯◯

JUMBLE®

Unscramble these four Jumbles, one letter to
each square, to form four ordinary words.

NOION

TECAN

LUDEMO

WLFOOL

Aaaaa! I can't believe this! Everything is ruined! How did this happen?

Hmm. I guess I didn't unplug the toaster.

WHEN HER FREEZER
STOPPED WORKING,
SHE HAD A ---

Now arrange the circled letters to form
the surprise answer, as suggested by the
above cartoon.

Print answer here

119

JUMBLE®

Unscramble these four Jumbles, one letter to
each square, to form four ordinary words.

DENUW

KUYCY

ALOTAF

PEDTIC

It's so beautiful out. I'm on a roll.

Welcome to Ann Arbor

THE PARKING
ENFORCEMENT OFFICER
WAS HAVING ----

Now arrange the circled letters to form
the surprise answer, as suggested by the
above cartoon.

Print answer here A 〇〇〇〇 〇〇〇

120

JUMBLE

Unscramble these four Jumbles, one letter to each square, to form four ordinary words.

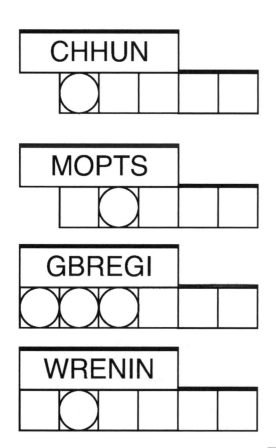

CHHUN

MOPTS

GBREGI

WRENIN

Wow! The kids are loving this.

Your son is swinging for the fences.

Happy Birthday!

EVERYONE AT THE PARTY THOUGHT THE PIÑATA WAS A ---

Now arrange the circled letters to form the surprise answer, as suggested by the above cartoon.

Print answer here

121

JUMBLE®

Unscramble these four Jumbles, one letter to each square, to form four ordinary words.

BAHIT

TURMS

CADEEF

SIMOWD

THE SPIDER'S
NEW BUSINESS
HAD A ---

Now arrange the circled letters to form the surprise answer, as suggested by the above cartoon.

Print answer here

122

JUMBLE®

Unscramble these four Jumbles, one letter to each square, to form four ordinary words.

OESOG

VURCE

KENAWE

MENARN

It looks like a tornado went through here.

THE CHILDREN'S BIRTHDAY PARTY TURNED EVERY SECTION OF THE HOUSE INTO A ---

Now arrange the circled letters to form the surprise answer, as suggested by the above cartoon.

Print answer here " ◯◯◯◯◯ " ◯◯◯◯

JUMBLE®

Unscramble these four Jumbles, one letter to each square, to form four ordinary words.

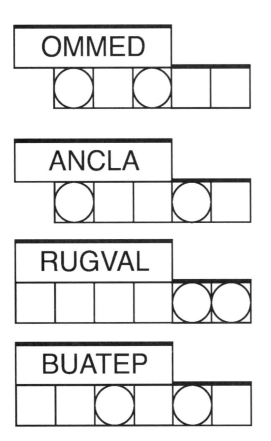

OMMED

ANCLA

RUGVAL

BUATEP

The previous owner barely drove it.

I'm getting a very bad vibe from this vehicle.

MAKE AN OFFER!

SHE DIDN'T BUY THE AUTOMOBILE BECAUSE OF ITS ----

Now arrange the circled letters to form the surprise answer, as suggested by the above cartoon.

Print answer here ☐☐☐ " ☐☐☐☐☐ "

JUMBLE®

Unscramble these four Jumbles, one letter to
each square, to form four ordinary words.

XSTIH

MULER

NIHLCC

GEREDE

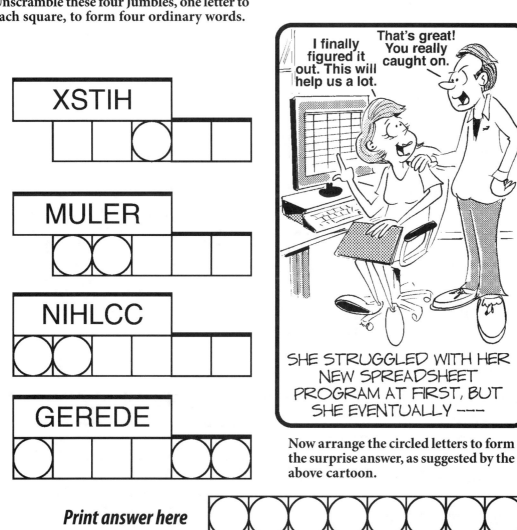

I finally
figured it
out. This will
help us a lot.

That's great!
You really
caught on.

SHE STRUGGLED WITH HER
NEW SPREADSHEET
PROGRAM AT FIRST, BUT
SHE EVENTUALLY ---

Now arrange the circled letters to form
the surprise answer, as suggested by the
above cartoon.

Print answer here

JUMBLE®

Unscramble these four Jumbles, one letter to
each square, to form four ordinary words.

CENUL

CEOTT

DIQUIL

DESEYP

Barbie, time
to get ready.

She should wear
this fancy dress to
the dance.

WHEN BARBIE WOULD
GO OUT ON A DATE,
SHE'D GET THIS.

Now arrange the circled letters to form
the surprise answer, as suggested by the
above cartoon.

Print answer here

JUMBLE®

Unscramble these four Jumbles, one letter to
each square, to form four ordinary words.

ASCEE

ETADD

EONCUP

NILEAH

RECORD STORES SELLING
BEATLES ALBUMS IN 1965
WERE FULL OF
PEOPLE WHO ---

Now arrange the circled letters to form
the surprise answer, as suggested by the
above cartoon.

**Print answer
here**

127

JUMBLE®

Unscramble these four Jumbles, one letter to each square, to form four ordinary words.

PEDUD

GUHOC

PAMIEL

SHLAPS

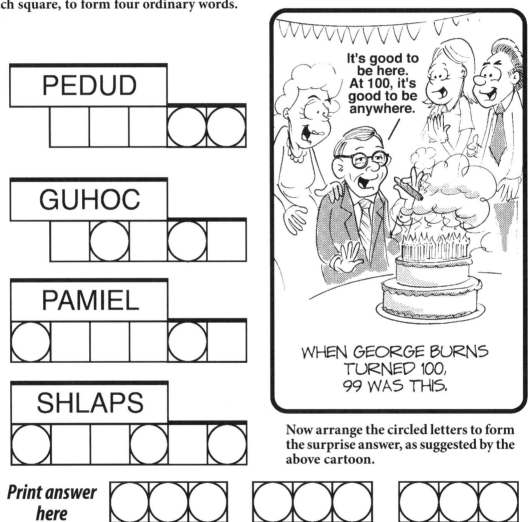

It's good to be here. At 100, it's good to be anywhere.

WHEN GEORGE BURNS TURNED 100, 99 WAS THIS.

Now arrange the circled letters to form the surprise answer, as suggested by the above cartoon.

Print answer here

☐☐☐ ☐☐☐ ☐☐☐

JUMBLE®

Unscramble these four Jumbles, one letter to
each square, to form four ordinary words.

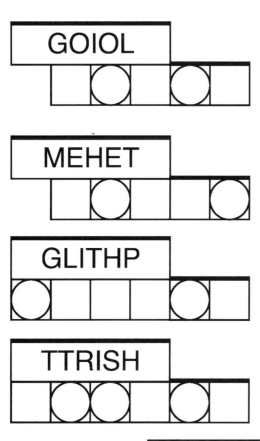

GOIOL

MEHET

GLITHP

TTRISH

Do you
think you'll
be able to
break any
altitude
records?

I'm going
to try.

WHEN IT CAME TO HIS
NEW HOT-AIR BALLOON
DESIGNS, HE HAD ----

Now arrange the circled letters to form
the surprise answer, as suggested by the
above cartoon.

Print answer here

Unscramble these four Jumbles, one letter to
each square, to form four ordinary words.

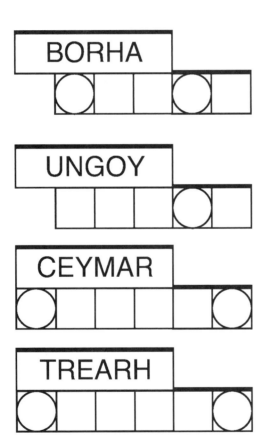

BORHA

UNGOY

CEYMAR

TREARH

How much longer
do you think it will
take until you're
all packed up?

AFTER HE ASKED THE
MOVERS A QUESTION,
HE SAID ---

Now arrange the circled letters to form
the surprise answer, as suggested by the
above cartoon.

Print answer here

130

JUMBLE®

Unscramble these four Jumbles, one letter to
each square, to form four ordinary words.

DOORE

XROPY

OUTPOR

WOWILL

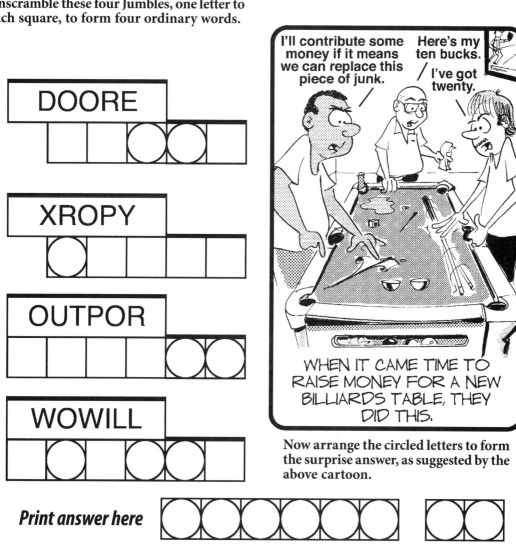

I'll contribute some
money if it means
we can replace this
piece of junk.

Here's my
ten bucks.

I've got
twenty.

WHEN IT CAME TIME TO
RAISE MONEY FOR A NEW
BILLIARDS TABLE, THEY
DID THIS.

Now arrange the circled letters to form
the surprise answer, as suggested by the
above cartoon.

Print answer here

JUMBLE®

Unscramble these four Jumbles, one letter to
each square, to form four ordinary words.

FUDIL

SUIES

ALOPPT

GLYTEN

This looks
delicious.

The decor
is so
luxurious.

ELEGANTES

THE CHEF'S NEW
RESTAURANT
WAS THIS.

Now arrange the circled letters to form
the surprise answer, as suggested by the
above cartoon.

Print answer here

JUMBLE®

Unscramble these four Jumbles, one letter to each square, to form four ordinary words.

TERIG

COSHA

FOCART

NICCIL

Brains?

Tickets.

WHEN THE ZOMBIES
TOOK OVER THE RAILROAD,
PASSENGERS
RODE ON ---

Now arrange the circled letters to form the surprise answer, as suggested by the above cartoon.

Print answer here

" ⬡⬡⬡⬡⬡⬡⬡ " ⬡⬡⬡⬡⬡⬡

JUMBLE®

Unscramble these four Jumbles, one letter to
each square, to form four ordinary words.

VEEKO

ZALPA

MACSUP

REEPIX

What's wrong?
Why aren't we
going?

THEY HAD NO CHANCE OF
WINNING THE BALLOON
RACE BECAUSE THEY
COULDN'T ---

Now arrange the circled letters to form
the surprise answer, as suggested by the
above cartoon.

Print answer here

JUMBLE®

Unscramble these four Jumbles, one letter to
each square, to form four ordinary words.

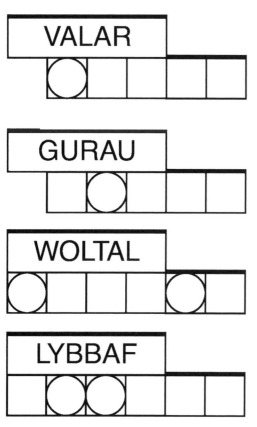

VALAR

GURAU

WOLTAL

LYBBAF

Not good
enough

Kings!

HOW THE POKER
PLAYER ENDED UP
WHEN HE WENT
ALL IN.

Now arrange the circled letters to form
the surprise answer, as suggested by the
above cartoon.

Print answer here

135

JUMBLE®

Unscramble these four Jumbles, one letter to
each square, to form four ordinary words.

DAITS

RUIFT

TAUROH

HOCCUR

How do you like it?

You're wearing a flower garden

WHAT HE
CONSIDERED
HIS WIFE'S NEW HAT.

Now arrange the circled letters to form
the surprise answer, as suggested by the
above cartoon.

Print
answer
here

" ◯◯◯ - ◯◯◯◯◯◯◯ "

JUMBLE®

Unscramble these four Jumbles, one letter to
each square, to form four ordinary words.

HERBT

DUIHM

CIMTRE

CHOPON

If I strike out
the side,
will you marry me?

WHEN THE BALL-
PLAYER PROPOSED,
IT WAS ---

Now arrange the circled letters to form
the surprise answer, as suggested by the
above cartoon.

Print
answer
here

A ◯◯◯◯◯ TO ◯◯◯◯◯

JUMBLE®

Unscramble these four Jumbles, one letter to
each square, to form four ordinary words.

NUBEG

GULAH

JELING

TALKEN

How do we get
out of here?

? ? ?

WHEN THE GUIDE GOT
LOST, THEIR AMAZON
ADVENTURE TURNED
INTO A ---

Now arrange the circled letters to form
the surprise answer, as suggested by the
above cartoon.

Print
answer
here

138

JUMBLE®

Unscramble these four Jumbles, one letter to
each square, to form four ordinary words.

WYLLO

WHOYS

BARJEB

DOALUN

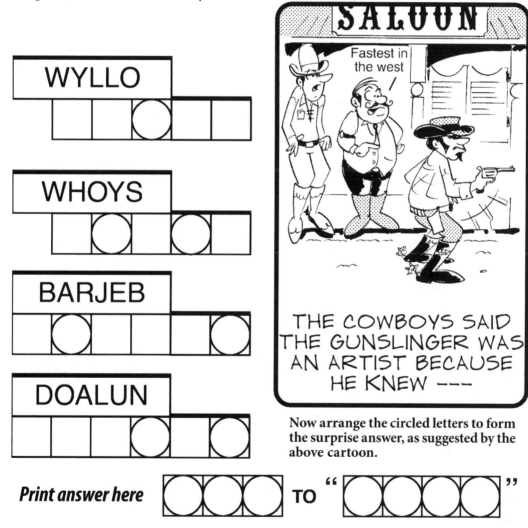

THE COWBOYS SAID
THE GUNSLINGER WAS
AN ARTIST BECAUSE
HE KNEW ----

Now arrange the circled letters to form
the surprise answer, as suggested by the
above cartoon.

Print answer here ◯◯◯ TO "◯◯◯◯"

JUMBLE®

Unscramble these four Jumbles, one letter to
each square, to form four ordinary words.

WEELJ

CIHRB

HERNID

NIEFED

They're not happy

Can we go now?

I'm tired

WHAT THE TOURISTS
EXPERIENCED IN
THE PARIS BISTRO.

Now arrange the circled letters to form
the surprise answer, as suggested by the
above cartoon.

*Print
answer
here*

JUMBLE®

Unscramble these four Jumbles, one letter to
each square, to form four ordinary words.

GODDE

SNKKU

VEIVER

FRAMIF

I love those
books!
Have you
read her
latest?

I've read
them all. Hi,
my name is
Clarice.

WHEN THE DOES MET,
THEY KNEW INSTANTLY
THEY WOULD
BECOME ---

Now arrange the circled letters to form
the surprise answer, as suggested by the
above cartoon.

Print
answer
here

" ⬡⬡⬡⬡ " ⬡⬡⬡⬡⬡⬡⬡

JUMBLE®

Unscramble these four Jumbles, one letter to each square, to form four ordinary words.

VUCER

OLPIT

SCINEK

PLOIWL

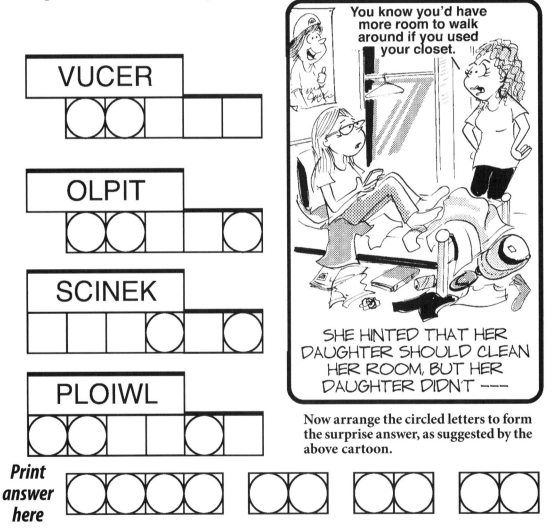

You know you'd have more room to walk around if you used your closet.

SHE HINTED THAT HER DAUGHTER SHOULD CLEAN HER ROOM, BUT HER DAUGHTER DIDN'T ---

Now arrange the circled letters to form the surprise answer, as suggested by the above cartoon.

Print answer here

JUMBLE®

Unscramble these four Jumbles, one letter to each square, to form four ordinary words.

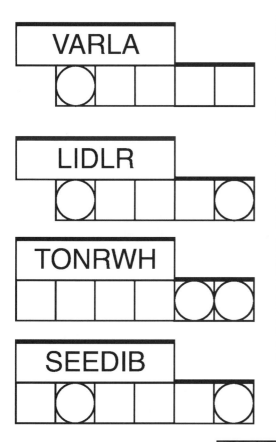

VARLA

LIDLR

TONRWH

SEEDIB

I'm sorry. It doesn't look good. At about 200 feet down we hit some rock that we just can't seem to drill through.

THEIR ATTEMPT TO DRILL FOR WATER DIDN'T ---

Now arrange the circled letters to form the surprise answer, as suggested by the above cartoon.

Print answer here

143

JUMBLE

Unscramble these four Jumbles, one letter to each square, to form four ordinary words.

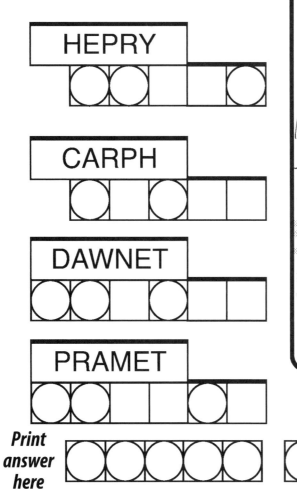

HEPRY

CARPH

DAWNET

PRAMET

Come on. I'm taking everyone out to celebrate!

AFTER HE PITCHED A PERFECT GAME, HE ---

Now arrange the circled letters to form the surprise answer, as suggested by the above cartoon.

Print answer here

144

JUMBLE®

Unscramble these four Jumbles, one letter to
each square, to form four ordinary words.

FUTLE

YATHS

WEREVS

MARDRO

Never worked
a day in his life

Sleeps all day,
parties all night

TO SOME, THE
BANKER'S SON WAS
WORTH A LOT, TO
OTHERS HE WAS ---

Now arrange the circled letters to form
the surprise answer, as suggested by the
above cartoon.

Print answer here

JUMBLE®

Unscramble these four Jumbles, one letter to
each square, to form four ordinary words.

DOREL

GOBEF

POOSUR

GROOFT

It's like walking
on marshmallows

WHAT A
COMFORTABLE
SHOE CAN BE.

Now arrange the circled letters to form
the surprise answer, as suggested by the
above cartoon.

**Print
answer
here**

⬡⬡⬡⬡ ⬡⬡⬡ THE ⬡⬡⬡⬡

JUMBLE®

Unscramble these four Jumbles, one letter to each square, to form four ordinary words.

WEHIN

HOCAP

TROIMP

SUFOAM

WHEN THEY RACED TO DEVELOP THE NEWS PICTURES, IT WAS A ---

Now arrange the circled letters to form the surprise answer, as suggested by the above cartoon.

Print answer here

"   "

JUMBLE®

**Unscramble these four Jumbles, one letter to
each square, to form four ordinary words.**

TYTUP

INVEG

NESIPP

SNIBAH

I'll need a big
loan, but this is
a good location

FOR SALE

WHAT THE EYE
DOCTOR REQUIRED
FOR HIS NEW OFFICE
BUILDING.

**Now arrange the circled letters to form
the surprise answer, as suggested by the
above cartoon.**

*Print answer
here*   A

JUMBLE®

Unscramble these four Jumbles, one letter to
each square, to form four ordinary words.

BEEOS

CONUE

REVDIR

FATCEF

HER GOLF SCORE WOULD
BE HORRIBLE AFTER SO
MANY OF HER SHOTS
WENT – – –

Now arrange the circled letters to form
the surprise answer, as suggested by the
above cartoon.

Print answer here

149

JUMBLE®

Unscramble these four Jumbles, one letter to
each square, to form four ordinary words.

ONLEV

YEDCA

RALNEY

LUTOWA

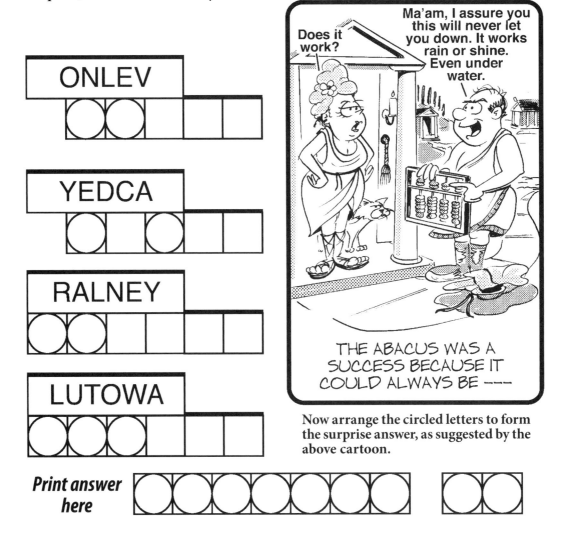

Ma'am, I assure you
this will never let
you down. It works
rain or shine.
Even under
water.

Does it
work?

THE ABACUS WAS A
SUCCESS BECAUSE IT
COULD ALWAYS BE ----

Now arrange the circled letters to form
the surprise answer, as suggested by the
above cartoon.

*Print answer
here*

150

JUMBLE®

Unscramble these four Jumbles, one letter to
each square, to form four ordinary words.

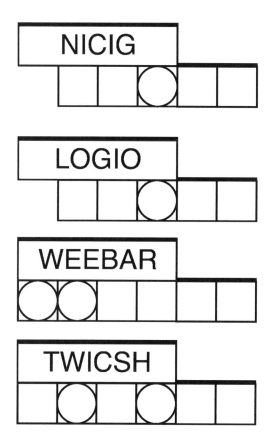

NICIG

LOGIO

WEEBAR

TWICSH

There must be some-
thing stuck in your
horn.

HE PRACTICED THE TRUMPET
FOR WEEKS BEFORE HIS
BAND TRYOUT, BUT ON THE
BIG DAY, HE ----

Now arrange the circled letters to form
the surprise answer, as suggested by the
above cartoon.

Print answer here

151

JUMBLE®

Unscramble these four Jumbles, one letter to
each square, to form four ordinary words.

ADOVI

SHACO

TEBNIT

GEEREM

Wow! You look
like you're doing
really well!

I'm thinking
of opening a
few more
shops.

CASPER'S NEW GHOST
COSTUME BUSINESS
WAS ---

Now arrange the circled letters to form
the surprise answer, as suggested by the
above cartoon.

Print answer here " ◯◯◯ - ◯◯◯◯ "

JUMBLE®

Unscramble these four Jumbles, one letter to each square, to form four ordinary words.

HAADE

SHYKU

PEPRAA

BEDULO

THE RABBIT'S COUSIN
WAS HAVING A ---

Now arrange the circled letters to form the surprise answer, as suggested by the above cartoon.

Print answer here

" "

153

JUMBLE®

Unscramble these four Jumbles, one letter to each square, to form four ordinary words.

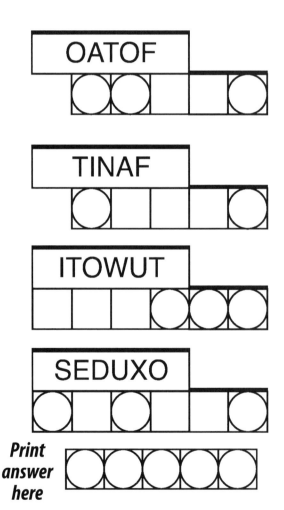

OATOF

TINAF

ITOWUT

SEDUXO

Ow! I didn't see that coming.

Well, Madam Futura did say you would be going "on a trip."

Crystal Clear Fortunes

SPRAINING HER ANKLE IN FRONT OF THE FORTUNE-TELLER'S SHOP WAS A ---

Now arrange the circled letters to form the surprise answer, as suggested by the above cartoon.

Print answer here

JUMBLE®

Unscramble these four Jumbles, one letter to
each square, to form four ordinary words.

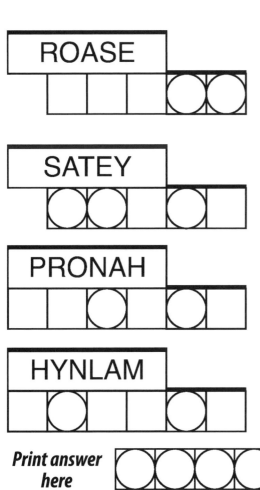

ROASE

SATEY

PRONAH

HYNLAM

These sugar-snaps are everywhere.

It takes very little time to fill the basket.

PICKING VEGETABLES IN
THEIR GARDEN
WAS ----

Now arrange the circled letters to form
the surprise answer, as suggested by the
above cartoon.

**Print answer
here**

JUMBLE®

Unscramble these four Jumbles, one letter to each square, to form four ordinary words.

ALFEB

TAIRO

GINSSA

YEMMAH

Gentlemen, I need you to man the front gate immediately.

THEY CALLED THE GENERAL BY HIS ----

Now arrange the circled letters to form the surprise answer, as suggested by the above cartoon.

Print answer here " ◯◯◯ - ◯◯◯◯ "

JUMBLE®

Unscramble these four Jumbles, one letter to
each square, to form four ordinary words.

NUBOD

LAZEG

CIMNOE

SOPLAT

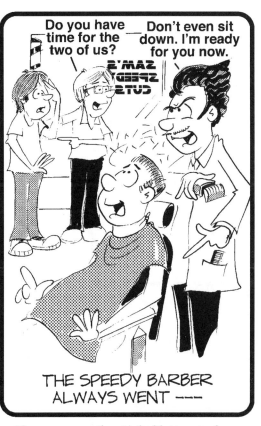

Do you have
time for the
two of us?

Don't even sit
down. I'm ready
for you now.

SAM'S
SPEEDY
CUTS

THE SPEEDY BARBER
ALWAYS WENT ———

Now arrange the circled letters to form
the surprise answer, as suggested by the
above cartoon.

**Print answer
here** AT A ⬡⬡⬡⬡ ⬡⬡⬡⬡

JUMBLE®

Unscramble these four Jumbles, one letter to each square, to form four ordinary words.

SHUBY

RILFT

RANWOR

NASCAV

THE MUSICAL KILLER WHALES FORMED ---

Now arrange the circled letters to form the surprise answer, as suggested by the above cartoon.

Print answer here AN " ◯◯◯◯ - ◯◯◯◯ "

JUMBLE®

Unscramble these four Jumbles, one letter to each square, to form four ordinary words.

GHEED

DAANP

WOOLLF

LIZTYG

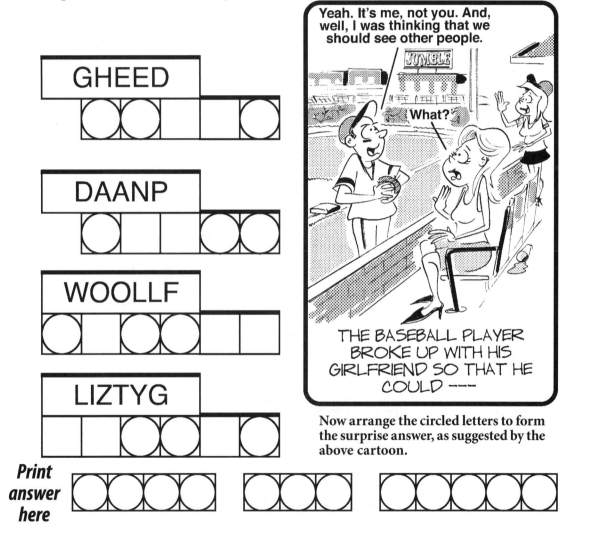

Yeah. It's me, not you. And, well, I was thinking that we should see other people.

JUMBLE

What?

THE BASEBALL PLAYER BROKE UP WITH HIS GIRLFRIEND SO THAT HE COULD ---

Now arrange the circled letters to form the surprise answer, as suggested by the above cartoon.

Print answer here

159

JUMBLE®

Unscramble these four Jumbles, one letter to
each square, to form four ordinary words.

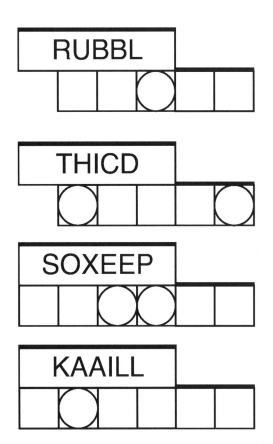

RUBBL

THICD

SOXEEP

KAAILL

Sorry.
I couldn't
find my guns.

I was about to do
this without you.

WHEN THE TRAIN ROBBER
WAS RUNNING LATE, HIS
PARTNER ASKED HIM WHAT
WAS THE ---

Now arrange the circled letters to form
the surprise answer, as suggested by the
above cartoon.

Print answer here

JUMBLE®

Unscramble these four Jumbles, one letter to
each square, to form four ordinary words.

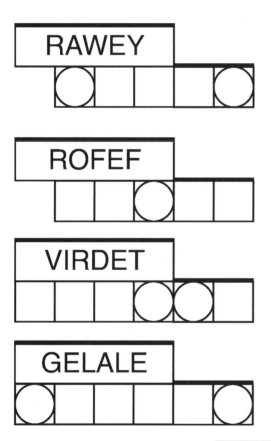

RAWEY

ROFEF

VIRDET

GELALE

$5 Toll
Cash Only

$5 Toll
Cash Only

$5
Cas

I thought
this would
be faster.

This is
going to
cost us time.

AFTER GETTING STUCK
AT THE TOLL BOOTH, THEY
WISHED THEY HAD
TAKEN THE ----

Now arrange the circled letters to form
the surprise answer, as suggested by the
above cartoon.

Print answer here

JUMBLE®

Unscramble these four Jumbles, one letter to each square, to form four ordinary words.

CIRKT

TIFAH

GINSEN

NURGPS

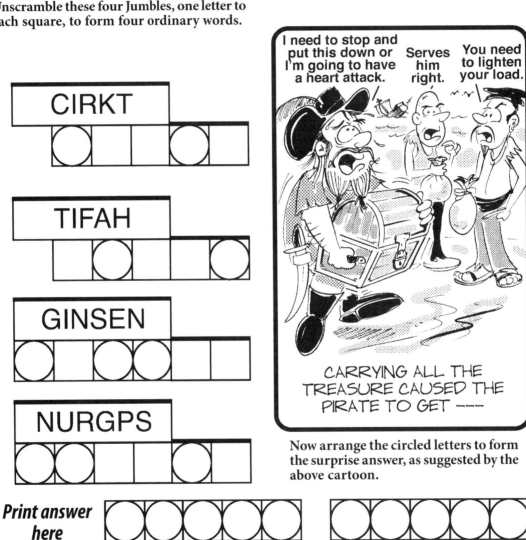

I need to stop and put this down or I'm going to have a heart attack.

Serves him right.

You need to lighten your load.

CARRYING ALL THE TREASURE CAUSED THE PIRATE TO GET ---

Now arrange the circled letters to form the surprise answer, as suggested by the above cartoon.

Print answer here

◯◯◯◯◯ ◯◯◯◯◯

Mystic
JUMBLE

Challenger Puzzles

JUMBLE®

Unscramble these six Jumbles, one letter to each square, to form six ordinary words.

YEKTUR

MUCAUV

GLOIBE

PUMITE

YASUNE

DOSTIL

SILENCE

WHAT THE LIBRARIAN'S LOOKS DID.

Now arrange the circled letters to form the surprise answer, as suggested by the above cartoon.

Print answer here ⬡⬡⬡⬡⬡ ⬡⬡⬡⬡⬡⬡⬡

JUMBLE®

Unscramble these six Jumbles, one letter to
each square, to form six ordinary words.

TULNAW

CUBDAT

MAIROH

NATQUI

LAGYAX

ROLARP

He won't pay

Take him in

TAXI

YOU'LL BE CHARGED
AFTER A RIDE IN THIS.

Now arrange the circled letters to form
the surprise answer, as suggested by
the above cartoon.

Print answer here A ⬡⬡⬡⬡⬡⬡ ⬡⬡⬡⬡⬡

JUMBLE®

Unscramble these six Jumbles, one letter to each square, to form six ordinary words.

YARVOS

GINDAR

BETASK

MIDYOF

VINTAY

LESUNS

On the house

On the house

On the house

HOW MUCH CAN A FREELOADER DRINK?

Now arrange the circled letters to form the surprise answer, as suggested by the above cartoon.

Print answer here

166

JUMBLE®

Unscramble these six Jumbles, one letter to
each square, to form six ordinary words.

ENMUIM

BEEDAT

PARTTE

HOMAFT

RARQUY

BOUTES

WHY THE BLOND
WOULD HAVE NOTHING
TO DO WITH
THE HIPPIE.

Now arrange the circled letters to form
the surprise answer, as suggested by
the above cartoon.

Print
answer
here

SHE WAS ⬡⬡⬡⬡⬡ **&** ⬡⬡⬡⬡⬡⬡⬡

JUMBLE®

Unscramble these six Jumbles, one letter to each square, to form six ordinary words.

POEQUA

THALLE

LUDSON

TELSED

MARFOL

YONTUB

HOW TO LEARN TO SING WITHOUT A TEACHER.

Now arrange the circled letters to form the surprise answer, as suggested by the above cartoon.

Print answer here " ⬡⬡⬡⬡ – ⬡⬡⬡⬡⬡⬡⬡⬡ "

JUMBLE®

Unscramble these six Jumbles, one letter to each square, to form six ordinary words.

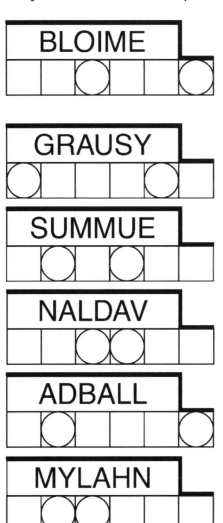

BLOIME

GRAUSY

SUMMUE

NALDAV

ADBALL

MYLAHN

This is old, Grandma

1988

I like the pictures

MARCH

THIS IS TRUE
NO MATTER HOW
LONG A CALENDAR
IS KEPT.

Now arrange the circled letters to form the surprise answer, as suggested by the above cartoon.

Print answer here

ITS 〇〇〇〇 ARE "〇〇〇〇〇〇〇〇〇"

JUMBLE

Unscramble these six Jumbles, one letter to each square, to form six ordinary words.

NOBBIB

YENITT

GIZZAG

SAYMID

TARPET

NECCIS

You sound awful. I quit

WHEN THE ANGRY CONDUCTOR WALKED OUT, THE ORCHESTRA FOUND IT---

Now arrange the circled letters to form the surprise answer, as suggested by the above cartoon.

Print answer here

" ◯◯◯ - ◯◯◯◯◯◯◯◯◯ "

JUMBLE®

Unscramble these six Jumbles, one letter to
each square, to form six ordinary words.

HIRAGS

DEECCA

PECILS

TELEEB

ENKORB

LIKLER

GET FLOSSING!

Open wide!

KENT

THE ARMY DENTIST
WAS KNOWN AS---

Now arrange the circled letters to form
the surprise answer, as suggested by
the above cartoon.

Print answer here

A " ⃝⃝⃝⃝⃝ " ⃝⃝⃝⃝⃝⃝⃝⃝⃝

171

JUMBLE®

Unscramble these six Jumbles, one letter to
each square, to form six ordinary words.

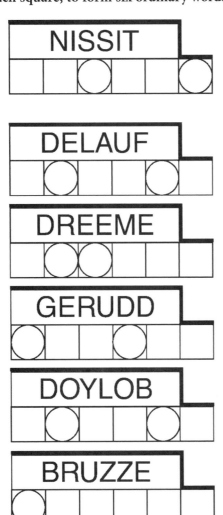

NISSIT

DELAUF

DREEME

GERUDD

DOYLOB

BRUZZE

I took out a loan
to keep them fed

WHEN THE RACE
HORSES KEPT
LOSING, THEIR
OWNER WAS ---

Now arrange the circled letters to form
the surprise answer, as suggested by
the above cartoon.

Print answer here

" ☐☐☐☐☐☐☐ " WITH ☐☐☐☐

JUMBLE®

Unscramble these six Jumbles, one letter to
each square, to form six ordinary words.

RAWHTT

ENGERE

EISORE

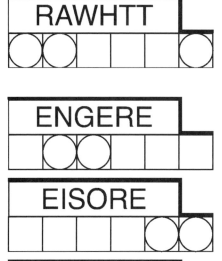

MOUFAS

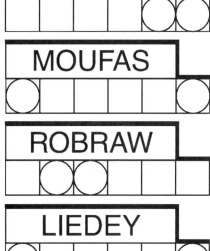

ROBRAW

LIEDEY

The $1,000 prize goes to...

WHAT THE WINNER
OF THE BIRD-
CALLING CONTEST DID

Now arrange the circled letters to form
the surprise answer, as suggested by
the above cartoon.

Print
answer
here " ⬡⬡⬡⬡⬡⬡⬡⬡ " HIS ⬡⬡⬡⬡

JUMBLE

Unscramble these six Jumbles, one letter to
each square, to form six ordinary words.

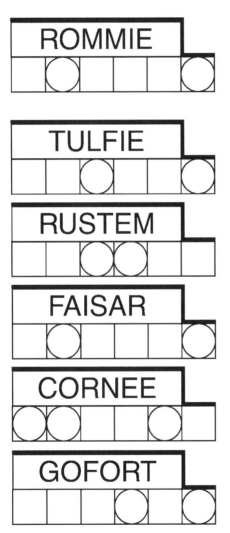

ROMMIE

TULFIE

RUSTEM

FAISAR

CORNEE

GOFORT

...and how's the family?

WHAT THE LOAN
SHARK TOOK WHEN
THE GAMBLER
PAID UP

Now arrange the circled letters to form
the surprise answer, as suggested by
the above cartoon.

Print answer here

JUMBLE®

Unscramble these six Jumbles, one letter to
each square, to form six ordinary words.

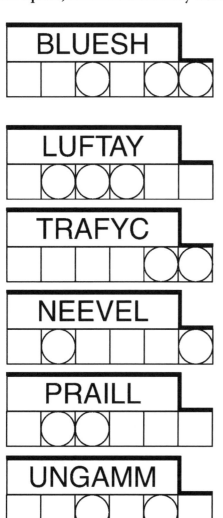

BLUESH

LUFTAY

TRAFYC

NEEVEL

PRAILL

UNGAMM

HAPPY BIRTHDAY!

How old are
you, Mom?

Old enough
to be your
mother

WHEN A WOMAN
STOPS TELLING
HER AGE, ITS ---

Now arrange the circled letters to form
the surprise answer, as suggested by
the above cartoon.

Print answer here

JUMBLE®

Unscramble these six Jumbles, one letter to each square, to form six ordinary words.

NERRED

CLAJAK

ETEELY

TELKAN

REPACT

DELBEH

WHAT THE MUSICIAN DID WHEN HE BECAME A POLICEMAN.

Now arrange the circled letters to form the surprise answer, as suggested by the above cartoon.

Print answer here

176

JUMBLE®

Unscramble these six Jumbles, one letter to each square, to form six ordinary words.

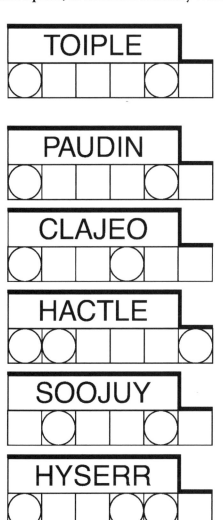

TOIPLE

PAUDIN

CLAJEO

HACTLE

SOOJUY

HYSERR

He was a real Casanova in college, your honor!

The thrill is gone!

THE CYCLE OF SOME MARRIAGES.

Now arrange the circled letters to form the surprise answer, as suggested by the above cartoon.

Print answer here

TO

JUMBLE®

Unscramble these six Jumbles, one letter to each square, to form six ordinary words.

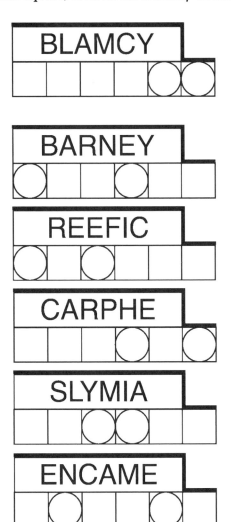

BLAMCY

BARNEY

REEFIC

CARPHE

SLYMIA

ENCAME

Careful where you step

OW!

THESE CAN MAKE YOUR FEET HURT WHEN VISITING ANCIENT RUINS.

Now arrange the circled letters to form the surprise answer, as suggested by the above cartoon.

Print answer here

" "

JUMBLE®

Unscramble these six Jumbles, one letter to each square, to form six ordinary words.

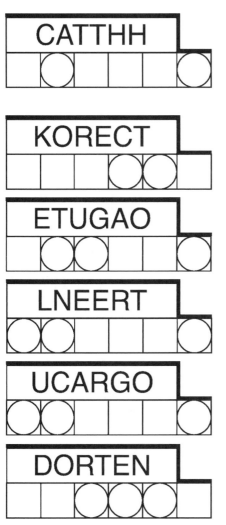

CATTHH

KORECT

ETUGAO

LNEERT

UCARGO

DORTEN

I don't know why he took that comment so personally...it was just a joke.

Man! He should have just let it go.

HE COULD HAVE AVOIDED GETTING PUNCHED IN THE FACE IF HE'D ---

Now arrange the circled letters to form the surprise answer, as suggested by the above cartoon.

Print answer here

⃝⃝⃝⃝⃝⃝ THE ⃝⃝⃝⃝⃝ ⃝⃝⃝⃝⃝

JUMBLE®

Unscramble these six Jumbles, one letter to each square, to form six ordinary words.

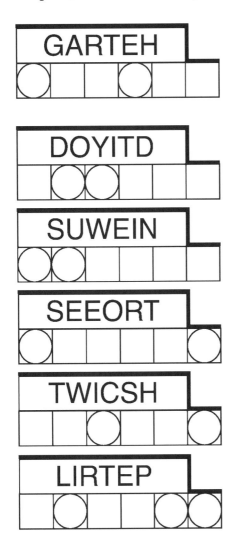

GARTEH

DOYITD

SUWEIN

SEEORT

TWICSH

LIRTEP

I am buying a whole truckload of soil. I should get at least a 25% discount!

I'm sorry. I just can't do that. This is premium potting soil.

TIP TOP SOIL

TIP TOP SOIL

TIP TOP SOIL

THE CUSTOMER DEMANDED A DISCOUNT ON THE POTTING SOIL, BUT THE NURSERY OWNER ---

Now arrange the circled letters to form the surprise answer, as suggested by the above cartoon.

Print answer here

180

JUMBLE®

Unscramble these six Jumbles, one letter to each square, to form six ordinary words.

RIMECT

ECAFAD

POYCUC

WUNNID

TETELK

RAHIOD

Daddy, this is Snake.

How's it going, Mr. C?

Have you ever heard of a haircut, son?

THE CYCLOPS WAS SUSPICIOUS OF HIS DAUGHTER'S NEW BOYFRIEND AND WOULD ---

Now arrange the circled letters to form the surprise answer, as suggested by the above cartoon.

Print answer here

JUMBLE®

Unscramble these six Jumbles, one letter to each square, to form six ordinary words.

GASHYG

PAIRIM

FTARYD

LECKAT

LEMWOL

DINNAL

Mom, I think I can dress myself.

Here, honey. You would look darling in this!

Young Miss

WHEN IT CAME TO FASHION, HER DAUGHTER WAS THIS.

Now arrange the circled letters to form the surprise answer, as suggested by the above cartoon.

Print answer here

"◯◯◯◯◯◯◯" - ◯◯◯◯◯◯

JUMBLE®

Unscramble these six Jumbles, one letter to each square, to form six ordinary words.

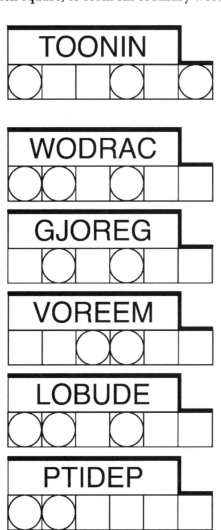

TOONIN

WODRAC

GJOREG

VOREEM

LOBUDE

PTIDEP

I think we can safely say that our new company will be a success!

It's a lock!

THE MERGER OF THE TWO SAFE COMPANIES WAS THIS.

Now arrange the circled letters to form the surprise answer, as suggested by the above cartoon.

Print answer here

A

Answers

1. **Jumbles:** YODEL BLESS IMPAIR SAFARI
   Answer: Where the gymnast found the music for her routine—ON THE FLIP SIDE

2. **Jumbles:** AMUSE DECRY HECKLE HYBRID
   Answer: What the guard did to the ship's intruder—HE DECKED HIM

3. **Jumbles:** CLOVE HAIRY RAREFY BEWAIL
   Answer: Another name for a giveaway—A "FREE" FOR ALL

4. **Jumbles:** BURST TOOTH BAMBOO METRIC
   Answer: Always on the car phone makes him this—A MOTOR MOUTH

5. **Jumbles:** GRAIN EVENT GOPHER FIESTA
   Answer: What attracted customers to the mattress shop—"SPRING" FEVER

6. **Jumbles:** ELUDE JUROR MALICE GEYSER
   Answer: A losing team can turn fans into this—JEER LEADERS

7. **Jumbles:** HITCH OPERA AFLOAT TRUISM
   Answer: What the rancher wanted from his herd—SHEAR PROFIT

8. **Jumbles:** EXPEL LOGIC COUPLE FALLEN
   Answer: How the trainer determined the fastest horse—WITH A GALLOP POLL

9. **Jumbles:** CRACK TITLE TAUGHT FAUCET
   Answer: What she considered her all-star fiancé—A GREAT CATCH

10. **Jumbles:** GAMUT ABIDE ELEVEN KILLER
    Answer: How the fishing shop attracted customers—IT LURED 'EM IN

11. **Jumbles:** ICING PATIO CONVEX ACTING
    Answer: What the happy-hour crowd considered the orator's remarks—INTOXICATING

12. **Jumbles:** APART CABLE JUMPER FACIAL
    Answer: Doctors try to avoid this—MALL PRACTICE

13. **Jumbles:** FELON UNCLE CELERY INHALE
    Answer: The best part of a soldier's morning—"ROLL" CALL

14. **Jumbles:** THICK UTTER ALWAYS BICKER
    Answer: He dreamed of millions but every week he received this—A REALITY CHECK

15. **Jumbles:** AGILE RUSTY BEYOND MALLET
    Answer: Athletes who learn humility often end up with these—ALTERED EGOS

16. **Jumbles:** CHUTE CLEFT ASSURE MELODY
    Answer: For the poker parlor almost nothing beats this—A FULL HOUSE

17. **Jumbles:** TYING HAREM ENMITY PUSHER
    Answer: What the bank got from its favorable yield offer—HIGH INTEREST

18. **Jumbles:** AISLE MADAM LIMPID BISECT
    Answer: What the lawmakers did at dinner—PASSED THE BILL

19. **Jumbles:** MERCY ARDOR FERVOR NEARBY
    Answer: What the boarder with the long reach became—BROADER

20. **Jumbles:** ESSAY ITCHY PRAYER EYELID
    Answer: What the lawyers called the flight update—"HERE" SAY

21. **Jumbles:** BROIL FEWER ACHING BECAME
    Answer: What mother said to the boy who had been playing with coal—WHERE HAVE YOU "BIN"?

22. **Jumbles:** EAGLE GUEST KINGLY SHOULD
    Answer: What was Dr. Jekyll's favorite game?—"HYDE" & SEEK

23. **Jumbles:** DOUBT PLUSH BROGUE SEAMAN
    Answer: What the male of the species was suffering from as he was about to get married—GOOSE BUMPS

24. **Jumbles:** MAIZE BAKED TYPING AMAZON
    Answer: Love may not make the world go round, but it certainly makes many people this—DIZZY

25. **Jumbles:** GOING HELLO SIMILE OUTBID
    Answer: What that ingratiating bald gentleman was—AN OLD SMOOTHIE

26. **Jumbles:** METAL CAPON BARIUM ACCEDE
    Answer: What the oyster did when asked where all his pearls were—HE "CLAMMED" UP

27. **Jumbles:** PRUNE BUILT LANCER GRISLY
    Answer: They always took their fat uncle along on drives because of what he had—A SPARE TIRE

28. **Jumbles:** RHYME BROOK EYELET AMBUSH
    Answer: Some people tell jokes and others do this—MARRY THEM

29. **Jumbles:** POUND HYENA WISELY MOSQUE
    Answer: When it comes to shoes, time does this—WOUNDS ALL HEELS

30. **Jumbles:** AIDED DAISY BEACON MOTHER
    Answer: If you don't succeed at first, you'll never get to this—SECOND

31. **Jumbles:** GORGE FLOOR BEHIND CRAVAT
    Answer: He bought a car without a horn because he didn't this—GIVE A HOOT

32. **Jumbles:** MAKER STOOP BLUING PEPTIC
    Answer: What the family who owned the sweater factory was—VERY CLOSE KNIT

33. **Jumbles:** THICK AGING FACILE ORIOLE
    Answer: A man, who doesn't mind admitting he's "all wrong" when he is, is this—ALL RIGHT

34. **Jumbles:** FATAL GAUDY CALMLY BUBBLE
    Answer: What the salesman said that bargain bed was—A "LULLA-BUY"

35. **Jumbles:** HEDGE CRUSH SPLICE PELVIS
    Answer: What he would be if he said what he thought—SPEECHLESS

36. **Jumbles:** CAMEO PAGAN SNUGLY MAMMAL
    Answer: Where do goblins live?—IN "GNOME" MAN'S LAND

37. **Jumbles:** ALBUM PATCH WEAKEN SCROLL
    Answer: The electrician turned ballplayer really could do this—"SOCKET" TO 'EM

38. **Jumbles:** INEPT PIPER JIGGER FABLED
    Answer: What the dentist whose income lagged behind his neighbor's decided he'd have to do—BRIDGE THE GAP

39. **Jumbles:** BRIBE GUILD ALPACA UNTRUE
    Answer: How to enjoy reading a horror story—"CURDLE" UP WITH IT

40. **Jumbles:** BLESS OUNCE TAWDRY COHORT
    Answer: How a nest egg must be feathered—WITH CASH "DOWN"

41. **Jumbles:** GLOAT CASTE ABLAZE TEACUP
    Answer: The members of the jury are supposed to "sit" until they do this—"SETTLE"

42. **Jumbles:** MAUVE HOVEL TRIBAL VESTRY
    Answer: Could be another name for erosion—SHORE LEAVE

43. **Jumbles:** BIRCH FLAKE ADJOIN SCRIBE
    Answer: What a monument in the park often really is—FOR THE BIRDS

44. **Jumbles:** GROIN POUCH AWEIGH UNLESS
    Answer: The only thing that kept him from making a fast buck at the race track—A SLOW HORSE

45. **Jumbles:** TWEET CLOTH GALAXY ENSIGN
    Answer: How a competent thief does his work—
    "STEAL-THILY"

46. **Jumbles:** PLUSH BISON QUIVER THRIVE
    Answer: What the customs inspector said the smuggler's
    case was—OPEN & SHUT

47. **Jumbles:** BASSO PIANO CIRCUS HEALTH
    Answer: What they called the fountain pen tycoon—
    HIS NIBS

48. **Jumbles:** FORCE LYRIC PRYING INHALE
    Answer: What the prude said miniskirts couldn't be worn
    for—LONG

49. **Jumbles:** TONIC LEGAL HELMET OPENLY
    Answer: Many a guy has been stung trying to get this—
    A LITTLE HONEY

50. **Jumbles:** TRILL HEAVY MOTIVE BROGUE
    Answer: How the miser held on to his dough—TIGHTLY

51. **Jumbles:** FABLE MAKER COMPEL INFLUX
    Answer: What the girl who's the picture of health usually
    has—A NICE FRAME

52. **Jumbles:** CROUP JOUST OFFSET PENURY
    Answer: What ladles do—SCOOP SOUP

53. **Jumbles:** DITTY COWER GRAVEN APIECE
    Answer: Ready to eat!—RIPE

54. **Jumbles:** DUNCE WAGER SCRIBE VERMIN
    Answer: This can produce a tight kind of feeling—
    A SCREWDRIVER

55. **Jumbles:** BARGE LADLE TIMING BODILY
    Answer: It's all it's cracked up to be!—THE LIBERTY BELL

56. **Jumbles:** JOLLY IMBUE TACKLE PITIED
    Answer: When open, it provides drinks—A BOTTLE

57. **Jumbles:** JINGO MOTIF SHANTY DEPICT
    Answer: When you might decide to change a date—
    AT MIDNIGHT

58. **Jumbles:** AISLE EXERT IMPUGN VACANT
    Answer: One thing you can say for being poor—
    IT'S INEXPENSIVE

59. **Jumbles:** CABIN GUIDE JUMBLE HELIUM
    Answer: How the magistrate who was playing truant in the
    park acted—LIKE A JUDGE ON THE BENCH

60. **Jumbles:** AGILE FELON BRONCO WHENCE
    Answer: What the model's job was—WEARING

61. **Jumbles:** DRYLY NOISE ALIGHT LICHEN
    Answer: These kids might make THE RICH LEND—
    THE CHILDREN

62. **Jumbles:** LEAVE MONEY WHALER AWHILE
    Answer: What the rake was turned into after he got
    married—A LAWN MOWER

63. **Jumbles:** FEWER PIETY DIMITY BENUMB
    Answer: Why the ram stopped in his tracks—
    HE SAW A EWE TURN

64. **Jumbles:** ALTAR ENACT BUTANE TWINGE
    Answer: You don't know if you're this—UNAWARE

65. **Jumbles:** WIPED AFTER MODISH NEARLY
    Answer: What he thought his wife's mother was—
    A MOTHER-IN-AWE

66. **Jumbles:** FETID LOGIC VANISH BRUTAL
    Answer: How modern housewives sometimes get rid of
    unsatisfactory dishwashers—THEY DIVORCE 'EM

67. **Jumbles:** ROUSE FATAL BEGONE FASTEN
    Answer: To fill a big man's shoes you wouldn't do this—
    BRAG ABOUT YOUR FEATS

68. **Jumbles:** GUILD STOOP ATTAIN DAMPEN
    Answer: For some people, weight lifting might mean this—
    STANDING UP

69. **Jumbles:** THINK FORAY SAFARI ACCESS
    Answer: This might be conspicuous in some underwater
    play—A STARFISH

70. **Jumbles:** EXILE FRAME ZINNIA AFLOAT
    Answer: What a Moroccan said to someone he hadn't seen in
    years—YOUR FEZ IS FAMILIAR

71. **Jumbles:** HENCE SWOOP ABUSED CACTUS
    Answer: The best thing to use for feathering your nest—
    CASH DOWN

72. **Jumbles:** HARPY TAKEN MISERY FAIRLY
    Answer: What the guy who claimed he could read women
    like a book must have been—A MYSTERY FAN

73. **Jumbles:** CLOVE ERASE LEGACY BEAVER
    Answer: How the reducing business is carried on—
    ON A LARGE SCALE

74. **Jumbles:** GULCH EXPEL ADJOIN DURING
    Answer: Stolen from a chicken farm—A "POACHED" EGG

75. **Jumbles:** USURP MERGE FLABBY JESTER
    Answer: Currently influential around the southeastern U.S.
    coast—THE GULF STREAM

76. **Jumbles:** SWISH LOONY KENNEL FIGURE
    Answer: Girls should never let a fool kiss them—or this—
    A KISS FOOL THEM

77. **Jumbles:** SIEGE RHYME DOOMED HEARSE
    Answer: How to put the boss in a good humor—
    DO THE DISHES FOR HER

78. **Jumbles:** GIANT LUNGE PLUNGE ACTING
    Answer: The kind of guys many gals look for—
    ENGAGING ONES

79. **Jumbles:** CRUSH PRUNE BLUING DISMAL
    Answer: When you're this it's easy to feel chipper—
    IN THE CHIPS

80. **Jumbles:** SUITE CROON MUFFIN POMADE
    Answer: What you sometimes get when you put two and
    two together—CURIOUS

81. **Jumbles:** OAKEN DITTO TRIBAL NUANCE
    Answer: The best way to tell a woman's age—
    WHEN SHE'S NOT AROUND

82. **Jumbles:** DICED GOUGE CLEAVE HOPPER
    Answer: EACH with a pain—ACHE

83. **Jumbles:** VIGIL SCARY DITHER TARTAR
    Answer: A dress should be this when it's attractive—
    DISTRACTIVE

84. **Jumbles:** BIPED YODEL VIRTUE CONVOY
    Answer: This leaves no one out!—EVERYBODY

85. **Jumbles:** LEAFY CIVIL DRIVEL MIDDAY
    Answer: What some dentists might give you—
    THE DRILL OF YOUR LIFE

86. **Jumbles:** ELOPE EJECT TRAUMA ENGULF
    Answer: He paid for his neighbor's new oak because he
    wanted to—"TREET"

87. **Jumbles:** GIZMO TEMPO EXPAND YONDER
    Answer: When it came to her home's new front entrance,
    she—"A-DOOR-ED" IT

88. **Jumbles:** UNWED PROWL AGENCY FRIGHT
    Answer: After selling their one millionth battery, everyone at
    the battery factory was—CHARGED UP

89. **Jumbles:** YAHOO ARROW PULSAR UNSEEN
    Answer: The steaks at the chef's top-rated restaurant were
    undercooked—RARELY

90. **Jumbles:** CRAZE FIGHT UPTOWN EXOTIC
    Answer: After he walked home the winning run, the
    pitcher—THREW A FIT

91. **Jumbles:** ASKED SOUPY FLORAL BUREAU
    Answer: The wrestler on the bottom was going to end up
    being a—SORE LOSER

185

92. **Jumbles:** EVENT TENTH EUREKA IMPALE
Answer: The astronauts on Mars dug for ice in an attempt to—UNEARTH IT

93. **Jumbles:** ETHIC STYLE ARMORY AVIARY
Answer: If the ocean were run by a corporation, then Poseidon could be the—"SEA" E.O.

94. **Jumbles:** BOSSY CLOTH KNIGHT FINITE
Answer: After having the flu for a week, she was—SICK OF IT

95. **Jumbles:** SWOON IMPEL DIGEST DENOTE
Answer: The erratic golfer was experiencing—MOOD SWINGS

96. **Jumbles:** HOIST PRICE MASCOT CLINCH
Answer: The owner of the successful bakery liked to show off her—PIE CHARTS

97. **Jumbles:** RELIC BOGUS CLOSET ADJUST
Answer: She tried to make a dent in her credit card debt, but she couldn't—BUDGE IT

98. **Jumbles:** VISOR CIVIL DRAGON RELENT
Answer: The gold mine turned out to be a bust, but thankfully, there was a—SILVER LINING

99. **Jumbles:** MERGE NIECE MIFFED LAVISH
Answer: When the cats waited to enter the amusement park, they stood in a—"FEE-LINE"

100. **Jumbles:** CHIDE LOBBY BORROW FUMBLE
Answer: When he saw the price of the hardwood, he was—FLOORED

101. **Jumbles:** CLAMP TWILL WICKED JARGON
Answer: The phone at the prison featured—CALL WAITING

102. **Jumbles:** TEMPT MONEY SHRUNK LUNACY
Answer: She thought the idea of eliminating the penny was—"NON-CENTS"

103. **Jumbles:** SHYLY WEDGE SYMBOL NIMBLE
Answer: When he reviewed the plans for the new water park, he presented a—SLIDE SHOW

104. **Jumbles:** KITTY USHER SICKEN ATTEND
Answer: The skunk knew exactly when to spray, because she had good—"IN-STINKS"

105. **Jumbles:** ABOUT ELUDE ALLEGE BODILY
Answer: He would be leaving the police station without being charged, thanks to an—"ALI-BYE"

106. **Jumbles:** SCARF ISSUE MEDIUM PRANCE
Answer: When the beauty pageant winner from the U.S. traveled, sometimes she would—MISS AMERICA

107. **Jumbles:** JOIST ABACK DOCKET CHOPPY
Answer: He hoped that becoming the circus tightrope walker would be a—STEADY JOB

108. **Jumbles:** SLASH RISKY SHROUD KITTEN
Answer: His poor judgment when it came to designing tank tops would cause him to—LOSE HIS SHIRT

109. **Jumbles:** PRUNE IRONY OUTAGE DROWSY
Answer: When he talked about the advantages of using a spear, he made some—GOOD POINTS

110. **Jumbles:** CEASE YOUNG SMOOCH WEAPON
Answer: The arrival of the new baby brought—MANY CHANGES

111. **Jumbles:** SENSE AGENT GARLIC ZEALOT
Answer: When it came to the twins, she was interested in the—SINGLE ONE

112. **Jumbles:** FLUTE JUICE MODEST SHRINK
Answer: The judge's portrait didn't—DO HIM JUSTICE

113. **Jumbles:** ZESTY THICK ADVICE MINGLE
Answer: He played chess in Prague with his—"CZECH" MATE

114. **Jumbles:** PETTY CREEK THEORY JOVIAL
Answer: The argument about the pizzas end with a—"PIECE" TREATY

115. **Jumbles:** MINUS AFOOT BALLET SKETCH
Answer: After the huge turkey dinner with the family, he was—"THANK-FULL"

116. **Jumbles:** GIANT VALET UNPAID MIDDAY
Answer: She hoped her new billboard would give her company one—AN AD-VANTAGE

117. **Jumbles:** ONION ENACT MODULE FOLLOW
Answer: When her freezer stopped working she had a—MELTDOWN

118. **Jumbles:** UNWED YUCKY AFLOAT DEPICT
Answer: The parking enforcement officer was having—A FINE DAY

119. **Jumbles:** HUNCH STOMP BIGGER WINNER
Answer: Everyone at the party thought the piñata was a—BIG HIT

120. **Jumbles:** HABIT STRUM DEFACE WISDOM
Answer: The spider's new business had a—WEB ADDRESS

121. **Jumbles:** GOOSE CURVE WEAKEN MANNER
Answer: The children's birthday party turned every section of the house into a—"WRECK" ROOM

122. **Jumbles:** MODEM CANAL VULGAR UPBEAT
Answer: She didn't buy the automobile because of its—BAD "CARMA"

123. **Jumbles:** SIXTH LEMUR CLINCH DEGREE
Answer: She struggled with her new spreadsheet program at first, but she eventually—EXCELLED

124. **Jumbles:** UNCLE OCTET LIQUID SPEEDY
Answer: When Barbie would go out on a date, she'd get this—DOLLED UP

125. **Jumbles:** CEASE DATED POUNCE INHALE
Answer: Record stores selling Beatles albums in 1965 were full of people who—NEEDED HELP

126. **Jumbles:** DUPED COUGH IMPALE SPLASH
Answer: When George Burns turned 100, 99 was this—HIS OLD AGE

127. **Jumbles:** IGLOO THEME PLIGHT THIRST
Answer: When it came to his new hot-air balloon designs, he had—HIGH HOPES

128. **Jumbles:** ABHOR YOUNG CREAMY RATHER
Answer: After he asked the movers a question, he said—CARRY ON

129. **Jumbles:** RODEO PROXY UPROOT WILLOW
Answer: When it came time to raise money for a new billiards table, they did this—POOLED IT

130. **Jumbles:** FLUID ISSUE LAPTOP GENTLY
Answer: The chef's new restaurant was this—TASTEFUL

131. **Jumbles:** TIGER CHAOS FACTOR CLINIC
Answer: When the zombies took over the railroad, passengers rode on—"FRIGHT" TRAINS

132. **Jumbles:** EVOKE PLAZA CAMPUS EXPIRE
Answer: They had no chance of winning the balloon race because they couldn't—KEEP UP

133. **Jumbles:** LARVA AUGUR TALLOW FLABBY
Answer: How the poker player ended up when he went all in—ALL-"OUT"

134. **Jumbles:** STAID FRUIT AUTHOR CROUCH
Answer: What he considered his wife's new hat—"HAT-ROCIOUS"

135. **Jumbles:** BERTH HUMID METRIC PONCHO
Answer: When the ball-player proposed it was—A PITCH TO HITCH

136. **Jumbles:** BEGUN LAUGH JINGLE ANKLET
Answer: When the guide got lost, their Amazon adventure turned into a—JUNGLE BUNGLE

137. **Jumbles:** LOWLY SHOWY JABBER UNLOAD
Answer: The cowboys said the gunslinger was an artist because he knew—HOW TO "DRAW"

138. **Jumbles:** JEWEL BIRCH HINDER DEFINE
Answer: What the tourists experienced in the Paris bistro—FRENCH WHINE

139. **Jumbles:** DODGE SKUNK REVIVE AFFIRM
Answer: When the does met, they knew instantly they would become—"DEER" FRIENDS

140. **Jumbles:** CURVE PILOT SICKEN PILLOW
Answer: She hinted that her daughter should clean her room, but her daughter didn't—PICK UP ON IT

141. **Jumbles:** LARVA DRILL THROWN BESIDE
Answer: Their attempt to drill for water didn't—END WELL

142. **Jumbles:** HYPER PARCH WANTED TAMPER
Answer: After he pitched a perfect game, he—THREW A PARTY

143. **Jumbles:** FLUTE HASTY SWERVE RAMROD
Answer: To some, the banker's son was worth a lot, to others he was—WORTHLESS

144. **Jumbles:** OLDER BEFOG POROUS FORGOT
Answer: What a comfortable shoe can be—GOOD FOR THE SOLE

145. **Jumbles:** WHINE POACH IMPORT FAMOUS
Answer: When they raced to develop the news pictures, it was a—PHOTO "FINISH"

146. **Jumbles:** PUTTY GIVEN PEPSIN BANISH
Answer: What the eye doctor required for his new office building—A SIGHT SITE

147. **Jumbles:** OBESE OUNCE DRIVER AFFECT
Answer: Her golf score would be horrible after so many of her shots went—OFF-COURSE

148. **Jumbles:** NOVEL DECAY NEARLY OUTLAW
Answer: The abacus was a success because it could always be—COUNTED ON

149. **Jumbles:** ICING IGLOO BEWARE SWITCH
Answer: He practiced the trumpet for weeks before his band tryout, but on the big day he—BLEW IT

150. **Jumbles:** AVOID CHAOS BITTEN EMERGE
Answer: Casper's new ghost costume business was—"BOO-MING"

151. **Jumbles:** AHEAD HUSKY APPEAR DOUBLE
Answer: The rabbit's cousin was having a—BAD "HARE" DAY

152. **Jumbles:** AFOOT FAINT OUTWIT EXODUS
Answer: Spraining her ankle in front of the fortune-teller's shop was a—TWIST OF FATE

153. **Jumbles:** AROSE YEAST ORPHAN HYMNAL
Answer: Picking vegetables in their garden was—EASY PEASY

154. **Jumbles:** FABLE RATIO ASSIGN MAYHEM
Answer: They called the general by his—"SIR-NAME"

155. **Jumbles:** BOUND GLAZE INCOME POSTAL
Answer: The speedy barber always went—AT A GOOD CLIP

156. **Jumbles:** BUSHY FLIRT NARROW CANVAS
Answer: The musical killer whales formed—AN "ORCA-STRA"

157. **Jumbles:** HEDGE PANDA FOLLOW GLITZY
Answer: The baseball player broke up with his girlfriend so that he could—PLAY THE FIELD

158. **Jumbles:** BLURB DITCH EXPOSE ALKALI
Answer: When the train robber was running late, his partner asked him what was the—HOLD UP

159. **Jumbles:** WEARY OFFER DIVERT ALLEGE
Answer: After getting stuck at the toll booth, they wished they had taken the—FREE WAY

160. **Jumbles:** TRICK FAITH ENSIGN SPRUNG
Answer: Carrying all the treasure caused the pirate to get—CHEST PAINS

161. **Jumbles:** TURKEY VACUUM OBLIGE IMPUTE UNEASY STOLID
Answer: What the librarian's looks did—SPOKE VOLUMES

162. **Jumbles:** WALNUT ABDUCT MOHAIR QUAINT GALAXY PARLOR
Answer: You'll be charged after a ride in this—A PATROL WAGON

163. **Jumbles:** SAVORY DARING BASKET MODIFY VANITY UNLESS
Answer: How much can a freeloader drink?—ANY GIVEN AMOUNT

164. **Jumbles:** IMMUNE DEBATE PATTER FATHOM QUARRY OBTUSE
Answer: Why the blond would have nothing to do with the hippie—SHE WAS FAIR & SQUARE

165. **Jumbles:** OPAQUE LETHAL UNSOLD ELDEST FORMAL BOUNTY
Answer: How to learn to sing without a teacher—"DUET-YOURSELF"

166. **Jumbles:** MOBILE MUSEUM BALLAD SUGARY VANDAL HYMNAL
Answer: This is true no matter how long a calendar is kept—ITS DAYS ARE "NUMBERED"

167. **Jumbles:** BOBBIN ZIGZAG PATTER ENTITY DISMAY SCENIC
Answer: When the angry conductor walked out, the orchestra found it—"DIS-CONCERTING"

168. **Jumbles:** GARISH SPLICE BROKEN ACCEDE BEETLE KILLER
Answer: The Army dentist was known as—A "DRILL" SERGEANT

169. **Jumbles:** INSIST REDEEM BLOODY FEUDAL DRUDGE BUZZER
Answer: When the race horses kept losing, their owner was—"SADDLED" WITH DEBT

170. **Jumbles:** THWART SOIREE BARROW RENEGE FAMOUS EYELID
Answer: What the winner of the bird-calling contest did—"FEATHERED" HIS NEST

171. **Jumbles:** MEMOIR MUSTER ENCORE FUTILE SAFARI FORGOT
Answer: What the loan shark took when the gambler paid up—GREAT "INTEREST"

172. **Jumbles:** BUSHEL CRAFTY PILLAR FAULTY ELEVEN MAGNUM
Answer: When a woman stops telling her age, it's—USUALLY "TELLING"

173. **Jumbles:** RENDER EYELET CARPET JACKAL ANKLET BEHELD
Answer: What the musician did when he became a policeman—LEARNED THE "BEAT"

174. **Jumbles:** POLITE CAJOLE JOYOUS UNPAID CHALET SHERRY
Answer: The cycle of some marriages—COURTSHIP TO COURT

175. **Jumbles:** CYMBAL FIERCE MISLAY NEARBY PREACH MENACE
Answer: These can make your feet hurt when visiting ancient ruins—FALLEN "ARCHES"

176. **Jumbles:** THATCH OUTAGE COUGAR ROCKET RELENT RODENT
Answer: He could have avoided getting punched in the face if he'd—TURNED THE OTHER CHEEK

177. **Jumbles:** GATHER UNWISE SWITCH ODDITY STEREO TRIPLE
Answer: The customer demanded a discount on the potting soil, but the nursery owner—HELD HIS GROUND

178. **Jumbles:** METRIC OCCUPY KETTLE FAÇADE UNWIND HAIRDO
Answer: The Cyclops was suspicious of his daughter's new boyfriend and would—KEEP AN EYE ON HIM

179. **Jumbles:** SHAGGY DRAFTY MELLOW IMPAIR TACKLE INLAND
Answer: When it came to fashion, her daughter was this—"CLOTHES"-MINDED

180. **Jumbles:** NOTION JOGGER DOUBLE COWARD REMOVED TIPPED
Answer: The merger of the two safe companies was this—A GOOD COMBINATION

Need More Jumbles®?

Jumble® Books

More than 175 puzzles each!

Jammin' Jumble®
$9.95 • ISBN: 1-57243-844-4

Java Jumble®
$9.95 • ISBN: 978-1-60078-415-6

Jazzy Jumble®
$9.95 • ISBN: 978-1-57243-962-7

Jet Set Jumble®
$9.95 • ISBN: 978-1-60078-353-1

Joyful Jumble®
$9.95 • ISBN: 978-1-60078-079-0

Juke Joint Jumble®
$9.95 • ISBN: 978-1-60078-295-4

Jumble® at Work
$9.95 • ISBN: 1-57243-147-4

Jumble® Celebration
$9.95 • ISBN: 978-1-60078-134-6

Jumble® Circus
$9.95 • ISBN: 978-1-60078-739-3

Jumble® Exploer
$9.95 • ISBN: 978-1-60078-854-3

Jumble® Explosion
$9.95 • ISBN: 978-1-60078-078-3

Jumble® Fever
$9.95 • ISBN: 1-57243-593-3

Jumble® Fiesta
$9.95 • ISBN: 1-57243-626-3

Jumble® Fun
$9.95 • ISBN: 1-57243-379-5

Jumble® Galaxy
$9.95 • ISBN: 978-1-60078-583-2

Jumble® Genius
$9.95 • ISBN: 1-57243-896-7

Jumble® Getaway
$9.95 • ISBN: 978-1-60078-547-4

Jumble® Grab Bag
$9.95 • ISBN: 1-57243-273-X

Jumble® Jackpot
$9.95 • ISBN: 1-57243-897-5

Jumble® Jailbreak
$9.95 • ISBN: 978-1-62937-002-6

Jumble® Jambalaya
$9.95 • ISBN: 978-1-60078-294-7

Jumble® Jamboree
$9.95 • ISBN: 1-57243-696-4

Jumble® Jitterbug
$9.95 • ISBN: 978-1-60078-584-9

Jumble® Jubilee
$9.95 • ISBN: 1-57243-231-4

Jumble® Juggernaut
$9.95 • ISBN: 978-1-60078-026-4

Jumble® Junction
$9.95 • ISBN: 1-57243-380-9

Jumble® Jungle
$9.95 • ISBN: 978-1-57243-961-0

Jumble® Kingdom
$9.95 • ISBN: 1-62937-079-8

Jumble® Knockout
$9.95 • ISBN: 1-62937-078-1

Jumble® Madness
$9.95 • ISBN: 1-892049-24-4

Jumble® Magic
$9.95 • ISBN: 978-1-60078-795-9

Jumble® Marathon
$9.95 • ISBN: 978-1-60078-944-1

Jumble® Safari
$9.95 • ISBN: 978-1-60078-675-4

Jumble® See & Search
$9.95 • ISBN: 1-57243-549-6

Jumble® See & Search 2
$9.95 • ISBN: 1-57243-734-0

Jumble® Sensation
$9.95 • ISBN: 978-1-60078-548-1

Jumble® Surprise
$9.95 • ISBN: 1-57243-320-5

Jumble® Symphony
$9.95 • ISBN: 978-1-62937-131-3

Jumble® University
$9.95 • ISBN: 978-1-62937-001-9

Jumble® Vacation
$9.95 • ISBN: 978-1-60078-796-6

Jumble® Workout
$9.95 • ISBN: 978-1-60078-943-4

Jumpin' Jumble®
$9.95 • ISBN: 978-1-60078-027-1

Lunar Jumble®
$9.95 • ISBN: 978-1-60078-853-6

Mystic Jumble®
$9.95 • ISBN: 978-1-62937-130-6

Outer Space Jumble®
$9.95 • ISBN: 978-1-60078-416-3

Rainy Day Jumble®
$9.95 • ISBN: 978-1-60078-352-4

Ready, Set, Jumble®
$9.95 • ISBN: 978-1-60078-133-0

Rock 'n' Roll Jumble®
$9.95 • ISBN: 978-1-60078-674-7

Royal Jumble®
$9.95 • ISBN: 978-1-60078-738-6

Sports Jumble®
$9.95 • ISBN: 1-57243-113-X

Summer Fun Jumble®
$9.95 • ISBN: 1-57243-114-8

Travel Jumble®
$9.95 • ISBN: 1-57243-198-9

TV Jumble®
$9.95 • ISBN: 1-57243-461-9

Oversize Jumble® Books

More than 500 puzzles each!

Generous Jumble®
$19.95 • ISBN: 1-57243-385-X

Giant Jumble®
$19.95 • ISBN: 1-57243-349-3

Gigantic Jumble®
$19.95 • ISBN: 1-57243-426-0

Jumbo Jumble®
$19.95 • ISBN: 1-57243-314-0

The Very Best of Jumble® BrainBusters
$19.95 • ISBN: 1-57243-845-2

Jumble® Crosswords™

More than 175 puzzles each!

More Jumble® Crosswords™
$9.95 • ISBN: 1-57243-386-8

Jumble® Crosswords™ Jackpot
$9.95 • ISBN: 1-57243-615-8

Jumble® Crosswords™ Jamboree
$9.95 • ISBN: 1-57243-787-1

Jumble® BrainBusters™

More than 175 puzzles each!

Jumble® BrainBusters™
$9.95 • ISBN: 1-892049-28-7

Jumble® BrainBusters™ II
$9.95 • ISBN: 1-57243-424-4

Jumble® BrainBusters™ III
$9.95 • ISBN: 1-57243-463-5

Jumble® BrainBusters™ IV
$9.95 • ISBN: 1-57243-489-9

Jumble® BrainBusters™ 5
$9.95 • ISBN: 1-57243-548-8

Jumble® BrainBusters™ Bonanza
$9.95 • ISBN: 1-57243-616-6

Boggle™ BrainBusters™
$9.95 • ISBN: 1-57243-592-5

Boggle™ BrainBusters™ 2
$9.95 • ISBN: 1-57243-788-X

Jumble® BrainBusters™ Junior
$9.95 • ISBN: 1-892049-29-5

Jumble® BrainBusters™ Junior II
$9.95 • ISBN: 1-57243-425-2

Fun in the Sun with Jumble® BrainBusters™
$9.95 • ISBN: 1-57243-733-2